A personal guide for the most important person in my life – ME

Numerology

A practical guide helping you to live your OWN Best Life
Open the book and FEEL self-empowered

Nanny A. van den Oever

Best Life Ltd

Best of Life

belongs to

---

given by

---

date

To my beautiful children

Bella, Felice & Max

with so much love.

My dearest wish is that you always

live your OWN Best Life.

ISBN: 978-0-473-21870-6

National Library of New Zealand Cataloguing-in-Publication Data
Oever van den, Nanny A., 1954-
Best of life : a personal guide for the most important person in my life / Nanny A. van den Oever.
ISBN 978-0-473-21870-6
1. Numerology. 2. Conduct of life. I. Title.
133.335—dc 23

Publishers: Best Life Ltd
74 Southampton Street
Sydenham
Christchurch 8023
New Zealand.
www.bestlife.co.nz

Printed by Toppan Printing Co (Aust) Pty Ltd, China

I would like to thank:

The many people who have crossed my path and have helped me to become the person I am today. Some were there for a fleeting moment, some for a little while, some for much longer and some for my whole life. You have all made a difference and I have learned from all of you. Especially the ones who have challenged me, who brought me out of my comfort zone, who made me face my fears. These human beings taught me a lot and helped me greatly to live my journey more consciously. Through the process I know I have become a much stronger individual. They have given me more confidence and greater belief in myself. I'm very grateful for all of it. It has resulted in great happiness.

Unexpected support, trust and belief in me came from Lyn Butterfield, which set the project of publishing this book on a roller-coaster ride.

I sent the manuscript to my editor Lesley Marshall, who did a sterling job. At times she questioned my writing and made me think again, which has produced a better content and improved the English grammar considerably.

Leesa Ellis is the outstanding talented designer and illustrator. She has much experience in book production. She understood the technical aspects of the book. She was always so helpful and her creative talent is very positive and imaginative. Her enthusiasm for this literary composition intended for publication was shown through her working long and patiently to get the result, I so envisaged for this book. She has given the book a unique visual signature.

Finally I want to thank my family and close friends. My parents for giving me life, bringing me up and for supporting me in all my endeavours. Especially over the last few years my family and friends have been a pillar of support, while I pursued with great tenacity, persistent effort and determination the publication of this book.

The last word to my children for their unconditional love and non-judgement. As a mother you are the very best I could wish for. The three of you are my true-love.

The Author

Nanny A. van den Oever is the founder of Best Life Ltd. Since 2006 she has helped people from all walks of life to live their OWN Best Life. She uses her skills as a life coach, numerologist and tarot reader. Her true passion is the science of numbers known as numerology. For many years now she has taught, researched and deepened herself in this truly magnificent study of the occult significance of number vibration.

She believes this has given her an insight into her own life and the lives of others. It has inspired her to pass these insights on to all the people she reaches and as a result she has assisted them in living their OWN Best Life. She would love to bring this science into the mainstream. She walks her talk and she has great capabilities in the emotional and intuitive fields. Her main focus is to live on the positive side of life.

She was born and bred in the Netherlands. She married and emigrated to New Zealand in her early twenties and made it her home. She discovered through life experiences how important it really is to feel free and to take ownership of your OWN Best Life. Eventually thirteen years ago, after a Louise Hay workshop, she became empowered and courageously decided to take responsibility for herself and to embark on her own journey with her three young children.

Her thirst for self-knowledge and understanding of life motivated her six years ago to start her own business and to serve others finding their OWN Best Life. She is a professional speaker and attends Body Mind Spirit Festivals. She gives seminars and workshops on self-empowerment and numerology. Normally she would give readings in the Arts Centre Market in Christchurch every weekend. This used to be her way to reach many visitors and locals.

In 2011 that all changed because of the many devastating earthquakes and aftershocks her home town has suffered. She is determined to help rebuild this garden city again and has signed

The Pledge, committing herself to stay in Christchurch and help rebuild the shattered city. She looks forward to the day she is able to enjoy the beautiful inner part of the Garden City once again. In the distant future after the completion of major renovations, the opening of the old heritage buildings that make up the Arts Centre will be the icing on the cake for her.

Christchurch will rise again, more beautiful and safe than ever before.

Contents

Section Two: Numerology

Inspirational Quotes and Poems

The Invitation

Your thinking decides your success in life

Reflect upon your present blessings

How to have succeeded in life

Dreams

Buddha

Confucius

Step by step

Speak all the good you know of everybody

Courage is the mastery of fear

Smile

A return to love

Individuality

A to Zen of life

A time for everything

Time

Remember

Life is a journey

You are unique

Desiderata

The way of life

No action, no result

Self-empowerment

Miss me, but let me go

Never discourage anyone

Best of Life is a book to keep for yourself
and give copies to those you love.

A Note from the Author

Our lives are precious and we are in charge of our own time and energy. As soon as we realise this we will start making better choices and we will find we go more straightforwardly in life. No matter the condition of your life, you can build a life of success.

Many people are stressed and commit themselves to tasks they don't really like doing. From a very young age we lose ourselves; we are dependent on our carers and somehow we forget what we want, what we came to do and what we are good at. We need to have tenacity and willingness to live our OWN Best Life.

It normally takes a very long time for most of us to become empowered in our own life.

Knowledge will play a major part in this. All our answers lie inside us and once we take the time to get to understand ourselves we will find that life starts to flow better. When we have the desire to live our Own Best Life we become happier and feel more in charge. We still encounter many challenges, but somehow we are better equipped to deal with them. We need to be who we are and have the wish to become our best self. There is no such thing as luck – you can make your own. However the key is to get started, and this book will help you do that.

Life needs to see contrast for growth, this sets in motion for us to experience change and that will make us strong in our own belief. Normally out of problems come questions and we start to look for answers, which must create better ways to improve our life. There is no need to know everything; to see improvements, just begin. You will find you learn by doing.

It doesn't matter what age you are, there will always be issues you have to deal with and try to solve. Life will always stay a learning journey, which is what it is meant to be. We never get it all done. As soon as one goal is reached, another presents itself. We need to extend ourselves to get the best out of our life. We need to live with intention. Life is an exciting experience and a privilege to experience in today's world.

It's hard to keep up with the numerous changes that happen around us every day. This places many demands on our time and energy. So it's important that we become vigilant around our life's purpose and direction.

Each and everyone must decide for themselves what is important. This creates self-esteem and optimism. What you think is what will determine your future. Many of us struggle, are unhappy and don't know what we really want for ourselves. It's important you take control of your thoughts.

When you have faith in yourself you can succeed in everything you wish for.

The well-known questions: Who am I? What is my purpose? and Why am I here? come back to us regularly in our life. The older we get the greater role they will play. We see life differently when we are a teenager, a young adult, in our thirties, forties etc.

In essence we stay the same, but what will be important to us and what we want from life changes. The better we understand ourselves and life itself, the more we will feel in charge.

Numerology will identify your place in the nine-year personal cycle and give you the detail for each year, month and day. Always the very important Universal energy must be taken into account as well. The Universal force concerns itself little for our individual energy. However if you work for cosmic good it will give harmony in your day and you find it shows through inner peace and making your hope a reality. When we develop true masters in ourselves and be one's own individual, we will find the Universal conditions are our helpers.

There is a great deal of information out there and we often get bombarded and feel overwhelmed. We are in dynamic changing times and there are many demands on our time and energy.

This book *Best of Life* will help you to put all this information in perspective and in some order.

You don't need to read the whole book to get your answer.

You can just randomly open the book and it will provide you with inspiration, to decide what to do and how to handle a delicate issue in your life.

Visually it will satisfy your soul. It will make your heart sing by just looking at the pictures.

You could simply decide to meditate on an inspirational quote or poem and let the words really sink in.

Always and every time it will provide you with an answer on your dilemma.

New Year's resolutions will start your action plan and it will all end with you celebrating at Christmas and looking forward to a new level the following year.

The old Science of number vibrations known as Numerology will provide you with direction and insight.

The philosophy will show you when it is the best time to do the important things in your own lifetime.

Numerology will also help you to better understand other people in your life. It can take the challenge and stress out of relationships, because you understand much better where others come from and why they do the things they do.

It will create interesting conversations with others, and a way to decide for yourself how true it all is.

The book will guide you for the rest of your life and help you to feel in charge of yourself.

The empty pages will help you to keep a record of important events in your life. This will make it easier for you to exactly recall information for future comparison or reference. Life tends to repeat itself.

It could even become a heirloom of your family's history of special dates and events.

The first section will:

- Start with New Year's resolutions – new goals, dreams and visions for the year to come.
- Focus on the whole of life – health, finances, careers, relationships, leisure, family, personal growth, spirituality and continuing education.
- Empower you to live your OWN Best Life. It will keep you focused and connected to your purpose and desired outcome for your life. This will lead to an improvement in the quality of your own life.
- Help you focus your attention on what really matters, so you live a more authentic life.
- Give you some understanding of how important it is that you make wise choices around your time and energy. You will realise that less is often more and that quality is far better than quantity.
- Remind you to look back at the year and celebrate how much you have accomplished and then help you look forward again to a New Year with new anticipation to make it your best yet.

The second section will:

- Look at the history of the science of numbers known as Numerology. The world is built on the power of numbers.

- Give some interesting analysis about numbers.
- Explain the characteristics of each single number, plus the master numbers eleven and twenty-two.
- Help you calculate how to find your best way to direct yourself in the days, months and years of both your personal and universal time frames.
- Give you the best personal and universal direction for the next nine-year period, plus details of the days, months and years.
- Outline your personal lucky day in any month of the year and the best period to execute important plans, plus give you ideas to help you to live your OWN Best Life. Try it out and see if you increase your luck. I would love to receive your feedback on this issue for research purposes. Thank you so very much.
- Outline your lucky colours and what stones to wear relating to your own birth number.

Finally, empty pages will be scattered throughout the book to write down your own personal notes. After each chapter in both sections you will read inspirational quotes or poems. The whole book is illustrated with beautiful pictures to help nurture your soul and lift your spirit.

My deepest wish is for you to be free, to be empowered, to have fun, to be happy and to live your OWN Best Life.

Introduction

Do you live your OWN Best Life?

Life is important, especially your own life. Life changes fast and we are on the brink of a new consciousness. Our spiritual development is of high importance. We need to understand ourselves and make informed choices. Our soul will always live, always be our unique self. It was there before we were born and will continue to exist when we die. Our soul is our unparalleled identity within and it is in each and everyone of us. Our soul is a positive energy – very wise, compassionate and full of love. We enjoy and understand its full measure when we are in non-physical form. All our answers to all our questions will come from here. No one can ever know how you feel – only you can. Let this feeling guide you to your OWN Best Life. Let the flow of your life assist you.

At the moment and for many years to come we will experience many changes in world climate, economic circumstances and political strategies.

Best of Life will give you optimism, empowerment, awareness of your own energy and how to best direct it, and insight into when the best time is to action your choices with the help of the science of numbers, Numerology.

The question Do you live your OWN Best Life? is highly important to every individual and deserves a big answer. Life is precious and I believe you should feel your best each and every day.

Best of Life will give you knowledge and help you with a plan of action to make you feel in charge, and this in turn will serve you in reaching your full potential. There are times when we don't feel great or we know someone else who is experiencing that feeling. This book will be a start to improving your wellbeing. Our happiness comes from knowing ourselves well. We need to create this happy feeling independently from another.

Best of Life will be your best friend and it will never let you down in your quest for living your OWN Best Life – guaranteed.

Notes

page 8

Section One

Living your OWN Best Life

Chapter 1

Welcome to the New Year, to the New You

The New Year is upon us and as always it is a wonderful time to think and decide what you would like to accomplish this year. You are the most important person in your life and it is of utmost importance that you feel happy. You must decide to become the person you want to be. Nobody can do this for you. You live your OWN Best Life. You must have a strong desire within yourself to live your Best Life.

Look for people you admire. Is it their style, determination, creativity, optimism or strength? I can guarantee you have this quality as well. It could be hidden but it will be there for you to find and nurture. All it will take is for you to acknowledge it and to start seeing how wonderful you are.

As always when a New Year starts we are more inclined to start new resolutions. I think it is of utmost importance to know what your own energies are and what universal ones you will experience for the year so you can know how to direct yourself in the best possible way. We all live the same time with regard to hours, days, months and years. If you look back in history you find many people who lived short lives, but at the same time they did accomplish a lot in their life. They lived the same twenty four hours in the day, that you and I live. We only need to think of the artist, inventor, engineer, architect, thinker and writer Leonardo Da Vinci and realise how true this is. He was a natural genius who used his time and energy well. His achievements are even more commendable if you take yourself to the times in which he lived and worked. A role model to keep in mind as we live and make our OWN Best Life.

We all have our own destiny to fulfil. We all need to be who we are. Your soul has all the answers to guide you, but you have to have the tenacity and willingness to be who you are and to live it each and every day. We will always meet problems

and obstacles. Life is to experience the contrast and it always will be. That way we grow and become empowered, and find our way to live our OWN Best Life.

It is possible to make great use of your time and I believe the better you get to know yourself the more directly you will go through life. It's important for you to realise what you don't want, because this opens the way to a clear mind and to a direct path in life. I suggest you compare it with having a map when you visit a foreign city. By using the map you will go straight to the museum, markets etc; without it you will get there as well, but it probably will take you most of the day. This means you waste a lot of that precious time we all live. I believe numerology will assist you with creating that map – that insight into both your own and universal energy – so you will travel through your life more in a forward line.

Getting to know yourself will give you control; more and more you will be making the kind of choices that will help you achieve what you want to in your precious life. You will become less interested in what other people think you should do or how you should lead your OWN Best Life. You make the selections; you decide what is best for you. No one can ever tell you how to do this. Some quiet time will be needed to tap into your passion and your soul. You're the only one who can feel yourself. These feelings will tell you very clearly if you are on track or if you have to make some changes and fine-tune the life you live. These feelings have everything to do with energy, and that is what numerology can help you with. The more you are in tune with your feelings the more your life will be synchronised. You will start to understand when it is the best time to do something and when to wait and show patience. All this will

help you greatly with the goals you set yourself to accomplish in this year, this decade and this lifetime.

We make many choices, set many goals and have new dreams. We start each day with many choices to make. Yoga, meditation or exercise? What shall I wear today? What shall I eat for breakfast? And so it goes on and on.

Begin taking the steps to bring happiness and satisfaction in your life. You are worthy – you have so much love, success, abundance and fun inside you. This year, start every day by telling yourself how wonderful you are, how precious your life is, and how much you love yourself. Nothing else matters, nothing else is important – just you feeling wonderful about you. That is all that matters in life. Everything will fall in place if you just feel great. Make this your most important New Year's resolution.

The better we feel, the better our position is to make some powerful requests. We must formulate these wishes well. We need to know exactly what we want. We also need to know when we would like this to happen, and over how much time. We need to be clear and specific about what we like in our life. We need to ask for what we want – otherwise how can we get it? It's time to write down three powerful requests for this year and then start this week to develop your plan how to move in the right direction to realise your goals. The responsibility for your life and your world is yours only. Nobody has forced life upon you. You make your own dreams; you create your OWN Best Life.

Control and violence has no place in your life. No one can decide your life, no one can live your life, and no one can change your life. If for whatever reason you are

not happy with your life, you need to make the changes. Your life is always up to you – no excuses. You must give credit to yourself and see within yourself your wonderful spirit, full of love and vitality. You also must respect every other human being because their spirit is just like yours, full of love and vitality. When you curse another, you curse yourself and the curse returns to you. You always receive what you give out yourself. It is not our place to judge another. When you come from a place of love your whole life will change. Socrates said it beautifully: if you know a thing is wrong, never do it, ever. We should never do injustice. Therefore we should never return an injustice. We should never do evil to anyone. Therefore we should never return evil for evil. To do evil to a human being is no different from acting unjustly. Plato writings, he was Socrates student.

This New Year let it be your year. You are in charge, you make the decisions. Numerology can help you with this, refer to section two, chapters 18 to 23. We all go through nine-year periods. Each year is specific in its characteristics. Every year is a passing stage. Time is very limited, so it is important we make good decisions about our energy. I personally find the knowledge very helpful and I do walk my talk.

I also find that it helps with understanding other people better. It will take the challenge out of a relationship if you have a better understanding of where they come from. Say, for instance, you are in a seven Personal Year and your partner is in a six Personal Year. Your partner is in a year where the family is very important. She/he has a sense of duty and wants to make life happier for the family, children and partner. She/he looks for love and approval from loved ones. You, however, are in a spiritual and sabbatical year and would rather be alone. It's your time to think and analyse and possibly you don't feel like doing anything that has to do with lots of people.

When both of you understand the reasons for the differences, year after year, the relationship will create more fun and happiness. You and your partner will talk about the differences in your personal timing, realising they are not permanent just a passing stage. The difference will add to the relationship. Each year we do work with new energies, experiences and people.

Mostly try to start each day with appreciation. Just be happy for a new day.

I wish you a Prosperous and Happy New Year.

Henry Thoreau said it beautifully:

Go confidently in the direction of your dreams!
Live the life you've imagined.

The Invitation

It doesn't interest me what you do for a living. I want to know what you ache for, and if you dare to dream of meeting your heart's longing.

It doesn't interest me how old you are. I want to know if you will risk looking like a fool for love, for your dream, for the adventure of being alive.

It doesn't interest me what planets are squaring your moon. I want to know if you have touched the centre of your own sorrow, if you have been opened by life's betrayals or have become shrivelled and closed from fear of further pain. I want to know if you can sit with pain, mine or your own, without moving to hide it or fade it or fix it.

I want to know if you can be with joy, mine or your own, if you can dance with wildness and let the ecstasy fill you to the tips of your fingers and toes without cautioning us to be careful, to be realistic, to remember the limitations of being human.

It doesn't interest me if the story you are telling me is true. I want to know if you can disappoint another to be true to yourself; if you can bear the accusations of betrayal and not betray your own soul; if you can be faithless and therefore trustworthy.

I want to know if you can see beauty, even when it's not pretty, every day, and if you can source your own life from its presence.

I want to know if you can live with failure, yours and mine, and still stand on the edge of the lake and shout to the silver of the full moon, "Yes!"

It doesn't interest me to know where you live or how much money you have. I want to know if you can get up, after the night of grief and despair, weary and bruised to the bone, and do what needs to be done to feed the children.

It doesn't interest me who you know or how you came to be here. I want to know if you will stand in the centre of the fire with me and not shrink back.

It doesn't interest me where or what or with whom you have studied. I want to know what sustains you, from the inside, when all else falls away.

I want to know if you can be alone with yourself and if you truly like the company you keep in the empty moments.

Notes

page 18

Chapter 2

Do you have a dream?

We all remember Martin Luther King's words, "I have a dream". His famous speech was delivered during a civil rights march in Washington DC. In his last speech, a day before his assassination, he said, "I've seen the promised land" – a place where everyone would enjoy freedom including Negroes. Martin Luther King's dream was that the people who lived in America would not be judged by the colour of their skin, but by the content of their character.

It's very important to have a dream in life. We only need to look at Susan Boyle to realise how important this really is. She decided to participate in a UK talent show on television and sang her song "I Dreamed a Dream". She went out of her comfort zone and faced her fears. This is the way we can manifest our dreams and desires. We all know this changed her life from ordinary to extra-ordinary. This is possible for everyone who lives their OWN Best Life and decides to do the things they need to do. You must have a dream to become your own best self.

I think it is very important to dream BIG in your life. This way you create your OWN Best Life without a doubt. We tend to drift in life if we haven't got a real purpose. Yet it's not easy to know what you want. Thousands of people live their life without

really knowing what they desire. We often think negatively about everything that goes on in our life. We judge ourselves constantly – I don't look good today, I'm not good enough, nobody loves me, I'm not worth it, I can't do that job. Once you believe in yourself everything will be possible.

First begin by being positive. You can do anything you set your mind to and must always work on stopping your limiting beliefs about yourself. For myself, I now think it's irrelevant what others say about me – I will not take anything personal any more. If others do not live up to my expectations so be it. It will make no difference to my day. Mostly we tend to make quick conclusions – why someone doesn't phone us back, why we didn't get the job, why someone makes no time for us.

For a well-lived life you need a specific purpose in your life, and once you know it you MUST decide to get it. For example, if you really don't like your work you need to start thinking what your dream job would be and what you need to do to get it. You must not just accept your situation. You need to become accountable for your choices in your life and get an organised mindset. Your answers lie inside you. Decide to find your own way; your heart will guide you. You need to spend time alone, make your own choices, live with the intention, because only you can decide how to go about making your dream a reality in your precious life.

If an opportunity comes up it is no good just to say, I'll think it over. Your indecision is weakness. Instead make a choice, don't leave it to chance, and this way you'll make dreams come true. A decision in your own mind to find or work on your dream will create a change and will help you to make that vision into a reality. Your desire and

your passion for your dream will create a flow in your life. Always follow the flow of life; try not to fight it. The flow will guide you and lead to joy and happiness. I have complete faith that my dream will become true in my OWN Best Life.

People who dream get what they want – we only need to look at the great leaders in our world. They often make quick decisions and they go after them with a great desire to make them happen. Barrack Obama made the decision to become President of America; he became organised and went after it with fortitude passion.

Successful people often have a number of the same characteristics. They all seem to be determined and persistent in making a single goal a reality. They all show energy and action. Nothing much in life is achieved from being lazy and negative. They are creative and go after opportunities or they create these themselves. They take one step at a time, but never stand still. They often are direct and show integrity in their interactions with others. They expect to be successful and often dream big. They have a belief in their own greatness.

My dream was to publish my book. I wanted this to materialise for the Christmas market to go into the New Year, the New You. This will be a great guide to motivate yourself to live your OWN Best Life. Thirteen years ago in May 1999 I did a Louise Hay workshop and it gave me the courage to change my life and to start creating my OWN Best Life. My book to me is the result of my self-empowerment, my confidence in my OWN Best Life.

As always I let numerology guide me and therefore I sent a query letter to Hay House Publisher in Australia in February 2010. In March I received an e-mail: yes, good idea, but they suggested I do it electronic. This is, however, not my dream, I want a book in my hand. I want you to be able to write in this book so it will motivate and assist you to create your OWN Best Life. I hope it will find its place next to your bed and that it will become your own treasured personal copy. I just need to give full expression to my passion and to my soul. I need to be who I am and do what I long for: publish my book. This creates great power within me, and my talents come to the front. I feel in complete harmony with my destiny, my path in this life. It feels so wonderful.

Within two days of the first email I get another one from Hay House in America. They are organising a Writer's Workshop for seven days on a cruise ship and you can win $10,000.00 towards publication of your book. I call this flow of life – it reinforces my absolute faith in the process. I know it is the next step, it will need my action, my quick decision, my organisation, my desire to make this vision of mine into a reality.

So I book the workshop that day. It is in June, which gives me two months to prepare. I don't win but I learn so much, I know I will end up with a book in my hand – it's my dream and I will not stop till I have achieved this wish. I can't control the future, but I can stay in the process and I know I will be supported. There will always be setbacks, obstacles and changes, but the flow of life will lead me to what needs to be done to have my dreams become a reality. I have belief and I know all is possible. The silver lining turned out to be even more satisfying, and more challenging as well – the decision to self-publish my book.

Another eventful year passed and finally the following year 2012 my book was, with the help of some very important key people, published by me. This book in your hand right now was my dream. It is an end product of a twelve-year period during which I was bringing up my three beautiful children. I know a new life will open up, with more dreams and goals to come. My children are young independent adults now and live their OWN Best Life. They create their own happiness and I see this as my true success in my life. I fully enjoy their company, and their unconditional love for me. I'm so grateful they choose me to be their mother in this lifetime.

Numerology also showed me the way. The year 2011 saw the end of a nine-year cycle for me and the contemplation of a new level starting the following year. In the first year of a new nine- year cycle, we stand at a crossroad, between the old and the future. There is a strong desire to move forward and to improve your situation. It is a very important year, that will lay down the groundwork for the coming nine year period.

My ultimate dream is to reach many people and to encourage them to live their OWN Best Life. The book will help with this and it will also help me to introduce the science of numbers to a wider public. The book is a tool to connect with me. I believe that once you start working with this science life will become clearer, your choices will be more direct, you will develop a better understanding of people, your challenges will be easier to manage and you will make better use of your own time and energy. When more people start seeing the benefit of this science more and more research will become available, which can only help to create more insight in our lives.

Summing it all up, you MUST decide to DREAM BIG, create the desire, organise your thinking and actions around it, and have complete faith in the process. Stay eager and positive with lots of enthusiasm. Never give up; there is no reason why you can't have or do what you want in your OWN Best Life. Have lots of fun on the way, because from this position you will create powerful and strong feelings. The flow of life will do the rest and will make your vision and dream a reality – guaranteed.

Your thinking decides your success in life

If you think you are beaten, you are,
If you think you dare not, you don't.
If you like to win, but you think you can't,
It is almost certain you won't.

If you think you'll lose, you're lost
For out of the world we find,
Success begins with a fellow's will
It's all in the state of mind.

If you think you are outclassed, you are,
You've got to think high to rise,
You've got to be sure of yourself before
You can ever win a prize.

Life's battles don't always go
To the stronger or faster man,
But soon or late the man who wins
Is the man WHO THINKS HE CAN!

Napoleon Hill

Notes

page 27

Chapter 3

What does personal freedom mean to you?

When you look up the meaning in the dictionary for personal freedom you find the following: the condition of being free or unrestricted, the power of self-determination, frankness, outspokenness, and the Four Freedoms – freedom of speech and religion, and freedom from fear and want.

In my own life personal freedom has been my biggest battle. It has taken me a very long time to become assertive, to stand my own ground, to become an individual and to realise no one can know better than myself what I'm good at and what I want from my life. I often felt I had to be the peacemaker – just do what was expected and keep others happy. This attitude created a lack of confidence and self-esteem in my life, which made it harder and harder for me to show my own worth. I often wanted to be just myself and valued for who I am. It took a lot of tenacity and determination on my part to change this way of thinking around and to become a self-assured human being who believed in herself. I still get tested at times, but I'm much better equipped now to deal with it.

At this stage in my life I experience personal freedom as the essence of life. I cherish it and protect my personal freedom. I also feel more comfortable with active and freedom-loving people in my life. By doing this you become more a human being in your own right and so does everyone else in your surroundings. I truly believe the best relationships are the ones where each person can develop as an independent individual. My life is for living, to be happy, to honour myself as a woman, to love and be loved, to take a risk and to enjoy my life. In the end I think that is all that will matter.

In the beginning of a New Year we often think how will we make this year our very best ever? We have this feeling of starting afresh. Our

thoughts will be very important in this process. Our life needs a vision to be successful. We often set ourselves new goals and are more determined to reach them at this time of year. But these goals will need our focus, and we must be vigilant not to despair or let go of them with any little – or even big – setback.

Every thought we think will create our future. So we must be in charge of our own mind. We must have belief in ourselves and know that we can do anything we set our mind to. We may fail, but we must try again and again till we succeed. Through all this effort we must maintain balance, harmony and peace in our life. We must set our sights high, expect more from ourselves and don't settle for anything less than our wish. This way we discover our true power. We realise it is safe to be ourselves, to speak up for ourselves, to stand our ground and not to give in. When we speak we notice how powerful our words are. We can do a lot of harm with our words, and yet we can do so much good as well. It is said that emotional violence is much worse to receive than physical cruelty. Once a hurtful word is said we can apologise, but the pain it causes will stay with the recipient.

We mustn't forget that a person who is involved in violent action is someone who is hurting deeply. A well-balanced, happy and healthy human being is incapable of hurting another. When we judge we participate in violence ourselves. We must allow ourselves to feel compassion instead of vengeance for those who harm another.

We must think clearly, express ourselves creatively and positively, and do what feels right, and then life will treat us well. We do attract what we think, so change your thoughts and that will change your life. When we focus on the positive things in our life we start to feel so much better. It is so important to be grateful for all that is.

This is especially evident when we have an accident. I tripped in the street and fell hard on the left side of my face. I instantly had a swollen lip, broken and loose teeth, and developed a black eye. My first thought was to see a dentist. My vanity came to the front. I didn't dare look at my face, expecting the worst. As it turned out the dentist was very helpful and has given me back my smile. I'm truly grateful for all the specialised people among us who help us each and every day to solve our problems and make our life happy. Everything I wear, eat and use every day has been made possible with the help of others.

We are all unique and have different passions. So let's put all our attention on what we are good at and that will lift our spirit. Your life is your own. Start making some powerful requests. What is important to you? What do you want to achieve in your life? What is your vision of your life? What is your passion? What makes you most happy?

Powerful wishes are clear and specific and show exactly what you want. If we decide to lose weight it's helpful to know how many pounds we'd like to lose. We should also decide by what time we expect to reach this goal. This makes us more committed, determined and focused. Our thoughts will also be very important. We are an energy, and it is possible that when you are heavy you take on someone else's problems or grief. It's wise to decide what belongs to you and what belongs to others. Every action has a cause that has an effect on you.

It's always sensible to focus our energy on the solution of an issue and not the problem. The more creatively we think the more hopeful we will be. Any setback will develop our character.

Never lose faith – the universe totally supports every thought and wish you have.

Ask and you will be given, or if you don't ask you don't get – a quote by Mahatma Gandhi.

There are many books to read about the life of Gandhi. I acknowledge the book *Gandhi Naked Ambition* by Jad Adams. Gandhi was the best known of India's leaders at the time of

independence. He was a man who refused to judge and this philosophy was central in his whole life. He never gave up his vision of truth and nonviolence. No other leader in the world has been worshiped and followed by so many millions in his nation of India. He behaved wonderfully towards people he did not know, but he wasn't a good role model as a husband and father. He also wasn't always easy towards his friends and supporters. Mahatma means "great soul", a name given to this guru. His family name is Mohandas Karamchand Gandhi. His true acolytes follow his strict eleven vows – "nonviolence; truth; non-stealing; celibacy; non-possession; body-labour; control of the palate; fearlessness; equal respect for all religions; Swadeshi (use of home manufactures, especially the spinning wheel); freedom from being untouchable". All eleven vows should be observed in a spirit of humility.

I believe our world would look different if all of us decided – at the same time would be best, of course – just to honour the very first vow, "nonviolence". For us to heal and eliminate violence there must be love. Just compassionate, unconditional love for our fellow human beings. We would have peace and tranquillity. We need to be free to be who we want to be; we can't change another, but we can be ourselves under all circumstances. It may not always be easy, but I'm convinced it is the best. Always choose happiness.

Life is intriguing and gives us many tests. Numerology certainly tries to help and guide us. The way you think will make a huge difference to your results. Always stay positive, find hope and follow your heart. Just be yourself, – your best is always enough – and start NOW.

Reflect upon your present blessings

Reflect upon
your present blessings,
of which every man
has many;
not on your past misfortunes,
of which all men
have some.

No one is useless
in this world
who lightens the burdens
of another.

Charles Dickens

Notes

Chapter 4

How free are you from your past experiences?

We all live our lives and have many experiences, good and bad. We form beliefs around these events, either negative or positive. Mostly it's the negative beliefs that have a big impact on our way we live our lives. If we were abandoned, made to think we were not good enough, if we don't belong, were not loved unconditionally or were thought of as not important, our self-esteem and self-belief would have suffered greatly. It helps to look back on your life at times and think about the negative events that have occurred during your childhood or during your life. This most likely would have influenced your decisions and your choices in life. I strongly believe that the contrast you experience helps you to act and wish for a happier life. You do your most growing when life is difficult, and that can make you finally decide you want a better life or just that you want to be in charge yourself and your own life.

There's no doubt you're a wonderful human being who deserves to be happy, to feel great, and who can live her or his life as she or he pleases. You have all the ingredients to do this.

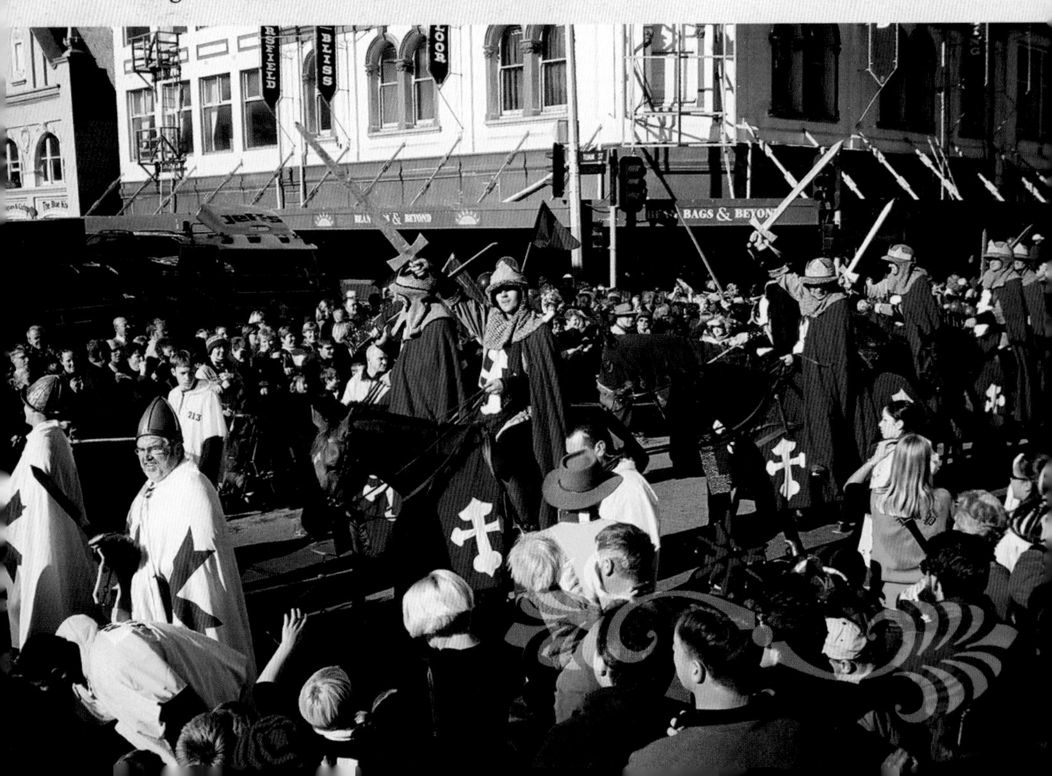

To go forward in life we need to uncover our negative experiences and feelings. We need to question how important and how useful they are to us today, whether to keep believing them or to let them go. Like everyone else I have experienced many difficult situations. My self-esteem and confidence suffered immensely.

Finally I started to love myself and to think of myself as a beautiful person. I made many changes, all for the better. It has been a slow but steady process to happiness. There is a blueprint of our life, but I know also that you always have a choice about how to decide to live your life. The choice will always be yours; never give your own power away to another. You will always know best. I'm positive that if you decide to end your own life prematurely, for whatever valid reason you have, you will be re-incarnated with a similar life and experiences. Every event or cause that has not yet fully produced its effect is something that still needs completion in the future. When there is an imbalance of energy it has to become balanced sometime and this will possibly not always happen in a single lifetime. Another reason why we live many lives. I do believe that you can't escape your responsibilities and duties. We learn from all the contrasts, experiences and decisions we experience in our many lives. You will hopefully make better choices next time and learn a better way to live your blueprint of life. You are infinite, with many, many possibilities and opportunities.

Not too long ago I had a big experience that made me sit up and question life again at another level. After the experience I looked for answers on various subjects and questions I have about life and because of that a greater insight in life has occurred.

I'd had a Reiki healing session and quite quickly I started to feel unwell. I somehow knew I was going to lose it and I wondered how long I could last. I became warm and asked for some water. I started slowly to lose sight and hearing. I stood up to go to the bathroom, but lost consciousness. I was put in the recovery position and I regained my awareness of life again. I felt good straight away; I had spilled my glass of water, but had no recollection of falling. An unusual experience and a bit frightening. After talking and thinking it through with several Reiki masters I realise now that on a soul level I had let go of some of my past experiences that I'd kept with me for a very long time yet had wanted to let

go for ages. It is possibly like a cleansing of karmic energy. It really confirms it to me how much energy we are.

We live in very special, often difficult times. The year 2012 heralds the end of an old era and the beginning of something new. We will experience the end of a 25,920-year astrological cycle and start a new one on 22nd December 2012. Due to a wobble in the Earth's axis, the zodiac appears to rotate, very slowly around the Earth. Sir Patrick Moore, a most respected astronomer, says in his book *Countdown! Or, How Nigh is the End?* that Earth is not a perfect sphere. It bulges slightly at the equator (the equatorial diameter is twenty-six miles greater than the diameter as measured through the poles), and the Sun and Moon pull upon this bulge, causing Earth to 'wobble' slightly in the manner of a gyroscope that is running down and has started to topple. The result is that the axis describes a small circle in the sky over a period of about 26,000 years. Obviously this alters the positions of the celestial poles, and hence also of the equinoxes.

An equinox is the astrological term for the time when the sun crosses the equator, making night and day of equal length in all parts of the world. When the sun is lowest in the sky and the nights are longest it's the winter solstice. The opposite happens when the sun is highest in the sky and the days are longest – the summer solstice. The spring and autumn equinoxes are midway between the times the sun is highest (summer) and when it is lowest (winter).The equinox dates for the Southern hemisphere (the half of the earth below the equator) and the Northern hemisphere (the half of the earth north of the equator) are always going through opposite seasons.

The central question of Moore's book – "Is there any chance that the world will come to an end?" – can be answered as follows, he says. The only tangible cosmic threat comes from asteroids or comets. However the dangers of collision are very low. Our greatest danger to mankind comes from ourselves. Nuclear bombs for example, yet if all the bombs now stockpiled were exploded at once the jolt would still be too slight to disrupt the Earth completely. However the crust might well be broken, resulting in major earthquakes, colossal outpourings of lava, tidal waves that would devastate the lands, and an atmosphere that would become strongly radioactive. The Earth would survive, but life upon it would not. So everything depends on politics – our leaders – who dictate our peace on this Earth. The Earth itself is in no danger, and will continue in its path until the sun destroys it, which will not be for thousands of millions of years yet. There is one certainty – the world will come to an end one day. But not yet.

Diana Cooper gives her views in her book *2012 and Beyond*. A new energy has already started to come into Earth in preparation for the upcoming changes. Energy is moving faster. You, like all the others – who are choosing to – must rise in consciousness so you will be ready for an extraordinary opportunity for spiritual growth. It has a lot to do with the alignment between Earth, the Sun and the Milky Way. Time will stand still for a moment. This is known as a cosmic moment, a time of the unknown and the miraculous, when things beyond human comprehension may happen. This offers the potential for a huge shift in consciousness and therefore we must use these high energies wisely.

The Mayan calendar also marks the end of a 5126 years cycle on 21st December 2012. They registered it like this 13.0.0.0.0. Their stone calendar started B.C 3114 recognized as the 1st day. It indicates the termination of one period of creation and the beginning of another. The ancient Mayan culture were very mystical people. I quote from a evening given by the Christchurch Gnosis Centre, part of the Association of Gnostic Anthropology.

> *We are certainly living in unpredictable times. The energy of the universe is unpredictable and mysterious. That's why I think it is important to make this day a day to remember. This special day, 21st December 2012. Make it your most important day for spiritual growth in your life. Whatever you decide to do this day, make it memorable. You may be alone, or with family or friends; maybe you could light a candle, pray, sing, play music, meditate, enjoy nature. But above all recognise the importance of this day.*

How to have succeeded in life

To laugh often and much,
to win the respect of intelligent people
and affection of children,
to earn the appreciation of honest critics
and endure the betrayal of false friends;
to appreciate beauty,
to find the best in others,
to leave the world a bit better,
whether by a healthy child,
a garden patch,
or a redeemed social condition;
to know even one life
has breathed easier
because you have lived,
this is to have succeeded.

Ralph Waldo Emerson

Notes

page 42

Chapter 5

The light at the end of the tunnel

It's natural for us to experience highs and lows in our lives. There would be no life if we didn't go through ups and downs. This is confirmed in our own heart graph – a straight line, there is no life. All my lows in life have been my turning points. They made me grow. I'm thankful for the lows. They certainly have made me think and helped me discover how precious life really is. Those are the times that we query life and ask ourselves big questions. We go in search for who we are, what we've come to do and what life means. Our answers are all within our own selves. We must learn to make both the good and bad times work for us; that way we are less worried and we develop a belief that we can survive anything.

There is such a thing as having faith, which is a belief you have. You just know it will work out in spite of the lack of evidence. I have found as I grow older that I can control my own personal highs and lows more. There are, of course, always outside events that happen and that I have no control over. I deal with those the best way I know.

First I always look for the hidden good in a time of darkness. This always helps me to create faith and this will lead then to hope. Faith is believing in something bigger then yourself, while hope just means a belief in yourself. Finding the hidden good will lift the darkness, the depression, and then I can discover my own ability to find ways to reach my goals. I believe that if you face your fear and you get out of your comfort zone, your fear will become less and less, and you will become more peaceful. In the process work on forgiveness, because you know that others are not responsible for your experiences; this way you gain power over yourself. I'm accountable and I need to fix my own issues.

How and what you think is of utmost importance. Believe in yourself, have faith in yourself and you can conquer everything. Once you stretch you can't go back to the old you. You will become more and more successful. Self-empowerment

gives great satisfaction in your life. Later when you look back upon your life you will always be more disappointed by the things that you didn't do than by the things you did. Your talents will come naturally to you in your life, whereas any skills you need in the process you must be prepared to learn. Together they will put you in charge of your life.

My emigration 35 years ago created expansion, excitement, and challenges like learning a new language and finding a job. At all times the hope for a higher quality of living was there. The darkness was leaving my family, friends and everything I had ever known and was familiar to me. The pain we experience in the dark times can wake us up. My divorce 13 years ago created freedom, independence, empowerment and time to develop myself. Still I experienced a huge sense of loss. That's why sometimes you need time to rest, to reflect and to renew yourself before the light can come in. It's important to give yourself time to recover. No one can ever feel you, so take time to be kind to yourself, to be your own best friend. I know that I needed this time for myself. I also know I used it well. It has been so productive for me, these last thirteen years. I truly got to know myself. I love my

own company and have experienced no loneliness. I have even come to a stage in my life when at times I protect my own time and energy. It can be so peaceful and energising to the soul to relish the simple quietness around you. It creates a feeling of pure happiness. Now that I'm ready to get back into life I will still always cherish my own time and space. I do create my own happiness and that is not dependant on other people. I have experienced this and know that now for certain. Yet sharing my life with others adds to the fulfilment of my life. There is so much love to give and receive.

Always in the bad times I return to basics and concentrate on what really matters to me. There is inner peace to be found this way, and through that I create a sense of strength. In the good times I'm happy and appreciate what I have. I try to stay realistic and keep working towards my vision. I celebrate every improvement, every little step closer to my ultimate dream. I know it is also a time to be wise and to prepare for the bad times that will come in the natural flow of life.

Every day I'm so grateful for my life. I live more and more in the moment, with a bird's-eye view to tomorrow and the future. I work on feeling great, whatever the circumstance. Happiness is to be found in the process, not just in the end result. Life is be lived and to be optimistic about. Life is really very short – we must put forward our best foot and know that everything always works out for the best.

We can change our life by changing our thoughts. We attract to us whatever we put our attention to – the cause-and-effect principle. We are always in charge of our OWN Best Life – without exception, without doubt. We have a part to play. So always expect only good things to come to you and they will.

Dreams

Water your dreams
with optimism and solutions
and you will cultivate success.
Always be on the lookout for ways
to turn a problem into an opportunity.
Always be on the lookout for ways
to nurture your dreams.

Being deeply loved by someone
gives you strength,
while loving someone deeply
gives you courage.

I have just
three things to teach:
simplicity,
patience,
compassion.
These three things are your greatest treasures.

When you are content to simply be yourself
and don't compare or compete,
everybody will respect you.

Knowing others is intelligence;
knowing yourself is true wisdom.
Mastering others is strength;
mastering yourself is true power.

Laozi or Lao Tzu

Notes

Chapter 6

Do you risk enough?

On the 8th of May 1977 I emigrated to New Zealand. I was born and bred in the Netherlands. I was 22 years of age and in my first year of marriage, and I didn't really know what I was in for. New Zealand was on the other side of the world. In lots of ways we were in free fall – no family, no jobs, no place to stay, and we had to speak a foreign language in daily life. We were looking for adventure, and certainly for a better life.

Life is about taking risks – feeling the fear and doing it anyway. We need courage to conquer our fear. Changes can be the catalyst of fear. It can certainly confuse us – rock our boat and confidence. However we must embrace change and trust it will bring us what we want to achieve. Life is change. So risks must be taken in our life. This keeps us in charge of change.

When we work with risk we open ourselves up to the possibility achieving what we want. If we like to move forward we need to sometimes go out on a limb. It's not always helpful to talk ourselves out of taking risks. Life will always change; we need to know and trust that at the same time it will support us. It makes you feel alive just to go for it, even if you don't know how it all will end. I believe we need to look before we leap. We need to plan and determine any possible obstacles. But there are times when we need to give up the old, to bring the new into our lives. I'm the only one who is responsible for my own life. To blame circumstances or people

for your situation doesn't do it. Claim your power; never give it away. Take charge, take a risk, but avoid too many impulsive ones because you could end up burning a bridge. Instead make sure the risks are calculated.

The challenges we experience today in this fast-moving Earth life often demand that we take risks. The tests help us to step out of our comfort zones and go for what we really want to do – to not settle for good, but to go after great. We can create our dreams and big goals this way. Often these days this happens not by choice, but through redundancy or losing our investments, or because of a natural disaster. Discover the silver lining; nothing happens without a reason. Never give up. I believe we need to dare to dream, even to dream big – not just to THINK things will get better, but to KNOW they will. There's always hope, I can assure you; just create the strong feeling of knowing it will, then concentrate on your wishes. Life will always bring everything you have asked for.

The following poem highlights the advantage of taking a risk. The author is unknown.

Risk

To laugh is to risk appearing a fool,

To weep is to risk being called sentimental,

To reach out to another is to risk involvement,

To expose feelings is to risk showing your true self.

To place your ideas and your dreams before the crowd

is to risk being called naive,

To love is to risk not being loved in return.

To live is to risk dying,

To hope is to risk despair,

To try is to risk failure,

The greatest risk in life is to risk *NOTHING.*

The person who risks nothing does nothing,

has nothing, is nothing and becomes nothing.

ONLY THE PERSON WHO RISKS IS TRULY FREE.

The better we feel about ourselves and the more love we have for ourselves, the more self-esteem and confidence we will have. To avoid taking a risk is to take the biggest risk of all. Conclusion: take the risks and start doing what you love to do; decide not to settle for anything less. Always know that your mind is capable of thinking out a plan of action and your physical self is capable of achieving your plan. Within you are all the tools you need to create your OWN Best Life. Ask for guidance and help and you receive it. As the saying goes – ask and you shall receive.

So decide today to go for it, take the risk; you'll never regret it, guaranteed. Start with deciding what you want, create the plan and take action. It will be a step-by-step process. Any failure is part of the plan; we can only learn by trial and error. Try again and again. Get back-up, do the learning, take the risk, and move forward towards your set goal. Life is a never-ending journey of contrasts; just always make sure you have lots of fun on the way. Life will never let you down. Decide you will and you'll be able to take the risk in your OWN Best Life.

Believe nothing
no matter where you read it,
or who said it,
unless it agrees with
your own reason
and your own common sense.

Be a light unto yourself.
Be your own confidence.

Health is
the greatest gift,
contentment
the greatest wealth,
faithfulness
the best relationship.

When you realise
how perfect everything is
you will tilt your head back
and laugh at the sky.

The thought
manifests as the word,
the word manifests as the deed,
the deed develops into habit,
and habit hardens into character.
So watch the thought
and its way with care
and let it spring from love.

Buddha

The way to happiness:
live simply, give much, fill your life with love.

Notes

Chapter 7

Live your best today – tomorrow will always be today

As the title says live your BEST today. Of course your best is not always the same. When you're happy it is quite different from when you're ill. Without exception, just do your best and know that's always enough. Tomorrow will on all occasions be today, because we will every time live in the NOW. We can plan and think about the future, but we will for ever live it in the moment. Age doesn't really come into it, unless you let it come through your thinking. There is no reason why you can't live an active life till the end of existence.

My view of life was confirmed a few years ago by a very special, inspirational woman. She was diagnosed in late July with a terminal illness. She was a very independent, private, courageous and loving person. She emigrated from the Netherlands to New Zealand in her twenties; she never had children, but lived very happily by herself for many years. She accepted her diagnosis and got on with organising her affairs. She was involved in many projects and organisations. She lived a very active

and full life. Anybody who was negative she gave the hard word to – she wanted to sing in the rain, receive a joke instead of a prayer. She still had many plans and was told she would live four months at the most. I have been privileged to be close to her in the last few weeks of her life. Before our eyes we saw her deteriorate more every day.

In times like these a book by Trudy Harris, RN titled *Glimpses of Heaven* can be very helpful to you. She says physicians who are "human" and allow their patients to remain "real people" even when they are dying play an enormous role in a person's ability to die well.

The book is full of final thoughts, words and visions from terminally ill and dying people. One was very profound and explained the power of God in an awesome way. She was sitting in a porch with a patient, who was quietly smoking his cigarette. He looked up at the wall facing him and, pointing to the famous picture of Jesus knocking on a door, asked her what it meant.

> *"The picture is of Jesus," I said, "and the door is to your heart. Jesus is knocking on it. Tell me what you see in the picture that is different?"*
>
> *Leaning as close to the picture as he could get, he said, "There is no doorknob on the door. Why is that?"*
>
> *"God is so gentle and tender with us. He will not force His way in," I said. "He wants you to open it from your side and invite Him in. The door has to be opened from the inside, by you. He only wants to come into your heart and make Himself known to you and take you to heaven with Him."*
>
> *"But suppose I just don't believe in Him at all, what then?' he asked.*
>
> *I suggested that he just tell God that he had never believed in Him and ask Him to please show him if He really exists. "Tell Him you're sorry for whatever you did wrong in your life, and ask Him to take you to heaven with Him, if that's where He is," I suggested.*
>
> *He smiled as we said goodbye, both of us knowing it would be for the last time.*

He died in the early hours of the next day. The nurse said he never moved and simply went to sleep peacefully. Later that day Trudy passed the porch where she had been the evening before. Not seeing the picture on the wall, she asked the nurse about it. The nurse reacted with surprise, saying there had never been a picture of Jesus on that wall. After carefully examining both the porch and the wall itself for nails marks or fading, Trudy

realised she was right. No picture had ever hung on that wall. Trudy was speechless, and so was the nurse.

On Friday 28th August, Daffodil Day, I bought a little book called *Eternity: Healing Quotations and Thoughts in Times of Sadness and Loss*. I opened the book for guidance that afternoon. The text was BE SWIFT TO LOVE AND MAKE HASTE TO BE KIND from author Henri Frederick Amiel and I knew I had to be quick to visit my friend. As it turned out I got to see her around four o'clock in the afternoon in her new apartment looking over the sea. Everything was just how she wanted it. She was very alert, peaceful and calm. She slipped away that evening at 20.30 p.m. and her watch on her arm stopped at exactly that time.

When you experience life so closely, be it a birth or a death, you change – and you appreciate everything so much more. Life is to be lived in exactly the way you want it. Nobody knows better than you yourself. We all make the same journey – we all are born and we all pass over. We are in charge of our lives. For us to look back on our lives and know we lived a well-lived life I believe we should keep Dale Carnegie's philosophy in mind.

Always have a positive mental attitude, and look for a major purpose in life to work on.

Keep sound physical health and harmony in all your human relationships.

Live with freedom in mind and be free of fear.

Always have a hope for achievement and let faith help you in the process.

Demonstrate a willingness to share your blessings.

Make your whole life a labour of love and service.

Keep an open mind on all subjects.

Use self-discipline to reach your goals and work on understanding people.

Last but not least, work towards financial security.

This will create choices and a way to do a lot of good in this world of ours.

To put the world in order,
we must first put the nation in order;
to put the nation in order,
we must put the family in order;
to put the family in order,
we must cultivate our personal life;
and to cultivate our personal life,
we must first set our hearts right.

When anger rises,
think of the consequences.

If you think in terms of a year,
plant a seed;
if in terms of ten years,
plant trees;
if in terms of one hundred years,
teach the people.

In regard to the aged...
give them rest;
in regard to friends...
show them sincerity;
in regard to the young...
treat them tenderly.

Kongzi or Confucius

Notes

page 60

Chapter 8

How to claim your power

Let's first look at who you are. You are a human being. You have a body and you are energy.

Energy attracts, so you are a magnet. Our lives get full with people and material items. Life takes over and we slowly feel we are losing control of ourselves. It becomes much harder to stay in control of our time and energy. There are so many demands from other people and our possessions that always seem to need more attention and management. It never is enough and we never get it all done. This means that there will be times in our life when we have to leave something behind to be able to move forward. Nothing should ever hold you back; no excuses are allowed.

It is always possible that we carry a problem or secret with us, but this is no reason to give up or stay stagnant. By keeping silent rather than exposing something, we decide to take the higher path. This way we create love and harmony instead of a blow-up and upheaval.

When you suffer of an addiction – eating food, sex, shopping, alcohol, smoking, drugs etc. – you must realise that this habit is not stronger than you. Part of your spiritual growth is acknowledging you have an addiction and that it is part of your journey to beat it and heal yourself. You must choose for yourself – to leave this part of yourself out of control or to do something about it.

It's important to know when it all started and to see with great clarity why you found this habit so attractive to begin with. Once you decide with certainty to challenge the addiction you can change your life around. You will become more grateful every day with your achievements. Always take it little step by little step. Address the painful feeling inside yourself and be firm with yourself not to escape into outside satisfactions such as smoking, eating etc. Keep challenging yourself and you will get better and better at it. Change your thoughts, believe in your strength and make a change in what you normally would do. Nothing is ever achieved in an instant. Everything takes its time, but know that you can beat this way of life. You are stronger than it, guaranteed.

Life is what you create. If you create a habit you experience it, if you create love you experience it, if you create anger you experience it, if you create fun you experience it, if you create a change you experience it, and so it goes on and on.

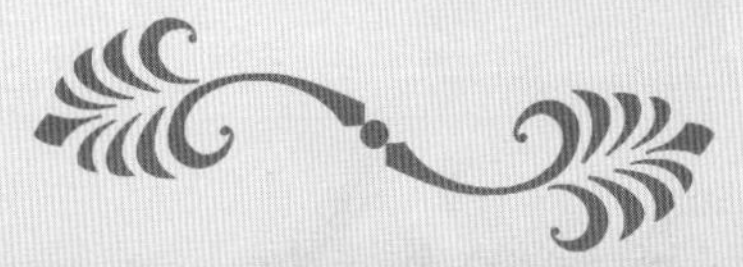

Your life is yours and it will be exactly how you decide it to be. Numerology can help you greatly with this as well. Sometimes you are stronger and sometimes you need more care and nurturing.

Numerology shows us that when we experience a personal year nine, month nine or day nine it is wise to let go, to take the learning, to finish our projects. Often in these periods people and/or material items can leave our life by our own making or out of our control. When we decide not to challenge these situations, we claim our power. Our intuition will always guide us.

In one of my nine-month periods I lost the office I had rented for 3 years, through circumstances outside of my control. I decided not to challenge it, to go back home and evaluate. In another nine-month period my two daughters – at the time 20 and 22 years of age – decided to leave home and become independent. It meant the end of an era for me. Life will never be quite the same again. I don't mean this is either negative or positive, it just is. I still live with my son at this stage; I cherish this and make the most of each day. When the time is right for him he will also leave, and I will ponder, Is my job done, or will it not be? I do think you always will be the mother. A job for life.

It is also good to see how Numerology can guide us. When I lost my office my landlord didn't phone me a month earlier or later. He made contact on the 2nd February, my start of the 9-month period. My girls told me in January a year later, again my 9-month time, about their wish to go flatting together.

We need to honour our own needs and desires to live our OWN Best Life. This will lead to liberation. We must show we love ourselves; we must show to ourselves that we are important in our own life. If your life is not giving you the results you want, if you know that you should do certain things but each time every day you don't do them, you need to ask yourself: How important am I? How can I improve this situation? What do I need to do? The answers are within you. Maybe you need to write a letter, lift your boundaries, become healthy, let go of a person in your life, etc.

Through meditation, natural breath rhythms and/or daydreaming we can transform our emotional and mental state and create a positive feeling in our lives. This will produce good vibrations and increase your productivity and your creativity. Life becomes happy and you will take your power back. We will always attract how we feel. A good way of doing this is to take time every day to bring back happy memories. If you recall unpleasant memories, put them into your mental rubbish bin and throw them out. It's as easy as that.

You are the only person who can make things happen in your life. You create your own happiness; never rely on others to do this for you or you will be disappointed. No one can ever live up to your expectations. You have so much more to give in life when you feel happy.

I advise you to look at your life and see what energies are draining you. Write it all down maybe you can do something about it in the future – or you can start right now. Identify the people, situations and material items at work and at home that are not helping you feel good. Begin with looking in your wardrobe for any clothes you never wear; give them away or recycle them. Also, every time you buy something decide to give something away. It's a way to keep control. If you have material items in your home that are a burden sell them on Trade-Me or give them to the Salvation Army or the City Mission. Take one drawer in the kitchen and see what items you can let go. You could be surprised. There's stuff there you probably never use.

Just to start is important; take little steps. Have lots of fun on the way. You'll notice at once that your energy lifts and you start to feel happier when you create control in your life and take your power back. At all times look after your body – give it good nutrition, water, exercise and plenty of sleep.

Step by step

The secret of making something work in your life is,
first of all, the deep desire to make it work:
then the faith and belief that it can work:
then to hold that clear definite vision
in your consciousness and see it working out
step by step, without one thought of doubt or disbelief.

Eileen Caddy

Notes

page 66

Chapter 9

How healthy is your own body?

When we live our OWN Best Life it is of great importance that we are healthy. Our body is our most important asset. We need to treat it well. We must take responsibility for our own health.

We must live our life in such a way that it will always be we who decide what we put into our bodies. Our bodies need every day special care.

Last year for the first time in my life I experienced an Ionic Detox Foot Spa. It is a pain-free approach to detoxing the body. You just put your feet in lukewarm water. An electrode connected to a computer gives a small current that pulls neutralised toxins out of the body into the water. After 30 minutes the water varies in colour and texture. This shows clearly the toxins that have come out of your body. This procedure can be of great benefit to you, especially after something like an invasive dentist treatment.

I am starting to believe the body can heal itself under all circumstances. Charlotte Gerson says that you can't heal selectively. Once you heal yourself, the whole body heals. All problems in the body will be gone.

Nutrition plays a very important role in this. Drugs don't really heal the body. They help to relieve pain and create a more quality life than otherwise would be possible. Good raw food should be a big part in any body's diet. Raw food should make up 51% of all the food you eat because it absorbs fast in our digestive system. How can we expect the body to live a long healthy life if we always eat processed, cooked and fast food? When we heat our food important vitamins will be destroyed; research has proved this.

Vitamins and minerals are of utmost importance. At times I do take some supplements, but the best way to get your vitamins and minerals is through food. When we buy good raw food we spend our money well. We invest in our bodies, and in our healthy future. Since the economic recession more people have created their own vegetable gardens. This way we are efficient and eat the most healthy foods. There is no time delay either – you eat while you harvest.

We also obtain this way a very important ingredient – chlorophyll. This agency captures sunlight to provide energy for the plants. Chlorophyll is the only substance known in nature that somehow possesses the power to act as a sunlight trap. As William L. Lawrence wrote in the New York Times, it catches the energy of sunlight and stores it in the plant. Without this no life could exist. We obtain the energy we need for living from the solar energy stored in the plant-food we eat or in the flesh of the animals that eat the plants. The energy we obtain from coal or oil is solar energy trapped by the chlorophyll in plant life millions of years ago. There will be a time when scientists will discover how man can live directly on solar energy.

Next, of course, is our need to drink water and lots of it. Dr. Marvin Kunikiyo in his book *Revolutionising Your Health* claims that ionised water is the solution to many of our health problems. It creates energy, radiant health and wellness in us. Since the earthquakes in Christchurch I have been getting my water from a spring. The water is so soft and delicious.

If you have any health problems in your life, improve your nutrition. I also highly recommend you to watch the DVD *Foodmatters*, and to do your own reading and research.

Your body is so precious and deserves special care and appreciation throughout your whole life.

Make it part of your normal rhythm of life to eat raw food, take some vitamin supplements, drink spirulina, eat cashew nuts and walnuts etc, eat dark chocolate (wonderful to know this is healthy), drink lots of water, and meditate. Think this information over and maybe start slowly and you will see the improvements in your life.

Write on paper what you do eat and how you feel. It will always be your own free choice, what you eat and what you won't eat. Malnutrition encourages you to be depressed. Problems like alcoholism and mental ill-health can be greatly improved through nutrition and vitamins.

I personally suffered thirteen years ago from terrible pains in my arms. It was a chronic pain, and part of my personal battle when I decided to leave my long marriage. I started the day with drinking two glasses of water when I first got up in the morning. After my shower and breakfast I would have another two glasses of water. I also took a multivitamin and 1000mg of vitamin C. During the day I ate raw nuts, dried prunes and fruit mostly. After dinner I would end the day with another two glasses of water and some calcium. This is an easy way to have your quantity of water a day. It took me four months to free myself of the pain.

Most days I still keep myself to this way of life. I hardly ever visit the doctor, except for routine check-ups. I value my body and take great care of what I put into it. I'm not a vegan or vegetarian. I like my food. I like quality before quantity. My mother – 85 years old – told me that the older she gets, she finds she eats less and needs less. Something to look forward to, maybe. It is definitely also my wish to grow old and to stay independent and to live a full, active, healthy life.

I'm sure that good nutrition, a vitamin supplement taken periodically, meditation and some regular exercise like walking will help with this greatly. If you're happy with your health and your body, all is well. If for whatever reason you know it could be better, look into your nutrition. As the famous quote says, "you are what you eat".

Change your food and you will change your OWN Best Life.

Speak all the good you know of everybody

Do not anticipate trouble,
or worry about
what may never happen.
Keep in the sunlight.

Remember not only to say
the right thing in the right place,
but far more difficult still.
to leave unsaid the wrong thing
at the tempting moment.

Be civil to all,
sociable to many;
familiar with few;
friend to one;
enemy to none.

The man who does things
makes many mistakes,
but he never makes
the biggest mistake of all ---
doing nothing.

Benjamin Franklin

ANTIGUA
BOAT SHEDS

Notes

JOHN JONES STEEL

KIA KAHA
CHCH ♥
merry Xmas

29

6.3M
QUAKE
2011
QUAKE
7.1M
CHCH 2010

KEEP
CALM
AND
CARRY
ON

Chapter 10

Creating happiness

My footpath sign has as title "Creating Happiness". I strongly believe that is what Numerology and coaching can give you. Before I decided to have this very important title on my sign I looked it up in the dictionary. What exactly does happy mean? The answer is a feeling of pleasure and a state of contentment. I like to stress the "feeling" of being happy. It comes from within.

I'm convinced happiness doesn't depend only on material goods, wealth, health or another human being. I'm sure that they all contribute to happiness, but real, lasting everyday happiness will always come through feelings from within. The state of being happy is not the same for everybody. I think we all have different keys; what is important to one is unimportant to another. The keys could possibly change over a lifetime as well – we change and grow as human beings and go through our four developments in life. I'm feeling the happiest I have ever felt in my life today and I attribute this to my three keys.

My first key is KNOWLEDGE. I don't mean the learning I have done at school and college, but my own self-development. Getting to know who I am – what is my purpose, my passion, my direction in this life and my ultimate goal. When I'm old I'd like to know: what does a well-lived life mean to me? The library is a most precious place to visit and borrow books to read from. The other day in the *Sunday Star Times* I read that New Zealand's prisoners are voracious readers – books like New Age, self-help and Harry Potter. How wonderful to learn there is hope for our society.

It has taken me a very long time to get to know my inner self and I'm sure there is a lot more to discover yet. I have a thirst for knowledge – finding answers to questions like: What is the meaning of life? and What am I here to do and to learn? Numerology is helping me greatly to get an insight into this. It's a very old science. It's practical, grounded and analytical and will always need research, but it's a blueprint, a character analysis, and it's so true and limitless. It's without question my true passion.

My second key is EMPOWERMENT. It's great to finally know what my passion, purpose and direction is, but dreaming doesn't give me true happiness. It's the acting upon my wishes and knowledge. You become in charge of your own time and energy and you gain self-esteem and confidence in life. You are in charge of your OWN Best Life. You become less interested in what other people think you should do or should be good at. I feel empowered when I decide to take action on my dreams. I don't believe in limitations or the finding of excuses; in my view anything is possible.

My third key is FREEDOM. We often feel fear, but I don't want to have thoughts about why I can't act upon my wishes and dreams. I don't want to make sacrifices for all sorts of good reasons, which end up being excuses most of the time. If you ask old people they will tell you to act upon your wishes today – don't wait for tomorrow or sometime in the future. Life is short and precious, as they have discovered. I'd like to be as a child – to feel no fear and experience life to the full, knowing anything is possible. It's often the adults in our lives who put the limitations in place and stop our true independence, creativity and freedom. Very often it becomes our life battle to beat our dependence created by the limitations that have been put upon us from a very young age. Life is often looked at from a place that demands us to be safe and not take risks, because there is a chance we might lose or get hurt.

At this stage of my life I have finally come to a place where I want to feel free and take opportunities, because I know now that potentially my thoughts and feelings

are limitless. We all must allow our genius to come out; we all are brilliant and amazing. I don't want rigid and dominant boundaries to decide what I can or can't experience. I'm ultimately only responsible for my own actions at any given time. I feel free and hopeful when I stretch myself and go out of my comfort zone. I have found this is the only way I can beat my challenges and deal with the weaknesses in my life. Following the flow of my life is the guide and it leads me to joy and to the deepest sense of who I am and how I wish to be. It creates the correct path to my true destiny.

And it all feels so right.

To sum it up, knowledge, empowerment and freedom have made a huge difference in my life. These keys have given me a real feeling of happiness. I'm only just on my way – I have many more wishes and dreams to put into place – but I know my three keys will continue to give me true happiness every day and all day.

I advise you find your own three keys and then act and live by them, and I guarantee you will find true happiness. Happiness is living your OWN Best Life. You'll know it and feel it when you do.

Courage is the mastery of fear

Courage is the mastery of fear –
not the absence of it.

Great people are those
who make others feel
that they, too, can become great.

Let us be thankful for the fools –
but for them, the rest of us
could not succeed.

The only way to keep your health
is to eat what you don't want,
drink what you don't like,
and do what you 'd rather not.

Drag your thoughts
away from your troubles...
it's the healthiest thing
a body can do.

Mark Twain

Notes

page 86

Chapter 11

What is important to you?

For you to live your OWN Best Life you need to know what is important to you. You have to create a vision. You have to know your values and passions. A value is something you feel strongly about or that is personally important to you. We all have values and they do direct our lives, though our values may change from time to time.

There will be a certain order in your values as well. We can put these in many categories such as personal, spiritual, lifestyle, image and power values. Your values must come from yourself – not because you wish to be liked or because you would like to please another person. You must always make your choices with your values in mind.

Think of it like this. When you plant a red rose seed in the ground you expect a red rose to grow and not a tulip. When our life does not produce the results we desire, we are doing something wrong. We are letting ourselves be influenced or manipulated, or maybe we're even punishing ourselves by not treating ourselves as special, worthy or important. We don't honour our values this way. So we must decide consciously to know ourselves well. For this to be realised we must ask ourselves questions.

Ask yourself: What is my personal value? What really matters to me? What do I like about myself? Is it my patience, helpfulness, reliability, organisation, good listening skills, hard-working habits, wisdom, playfulness, independence, freedom, relaxed nature, self-respect, confidence, energy, stamina, sense of humour, love, decisiveness, knowledgeableness, originality, kindness, or for being a great friend? And on and on it goes...

For my spiritual values I ask myself: Do I like to have a spiritual focus or inspiration in my life? Is faith important in my life? Will I practise meditation or will I participate in religion? Maybe I have no particular spiritual focus. I decide it's up to me to make the most of my life. My life is not limited to my five senses – hearing, sight, taste, smell and touch. What about my intuition? I know there is more than the realm of time, space and matter.

For lifestyle values I need to know: Do I want a quiet life, busy life or simple life? Do I work to achieve wealth, security, status? Will I raise a family? Have a beautiful home? Will the family come first or will I work towards a balance of home and work? Will I have a few or lots of friends? Do I want to make a contribution to society? Will I save or spend money? Will I invest in education, hobbies or personal development?

For image values: How do I want to be seen? Being popular, well-known, a strong person, talented, adventurous, kind, helpful, a high achiever, a great parent, an expert in a certain field, or just what you see is what you get?

For power values I would look at things that make me feel empowered. This can be as simple as looking good, having money, being competent, feeling healthy, enjoying the freedom to make my own decisions, believing in myself, having self-discipline or being highly skilled.

For myself, my own values are of utmost importance. They direct my life in a significant way. My goals are orientated around my most important values. I never lose sight of them when I make choices or important decisions.

My top value is knowledge and wisdom. I also value very highly my communication skills and my ability to use creativity to bring my message over clearly. In regards to spirituality I look for answers through my great passion, Numerology. I look for ways to explain the unexplainable and to understand this universe of ours. My family is of great value to me and I always work towards establishing happy, peaceful and harmonious relationships. Finally the freedom to be me – to travel, exploring new cultures and being of service – is an important value to me.

When we consistently find harmony in body, mind & spirit we experience a real sense of value. Our lives become enriched. We need to develop the spirit and look after our physical body at the same time. When we lack rest our body suffers. Our quality of life diminishes. You are responsible for what you do to your body. If you ignore the signs, you must pay the price. That is the natural law of cause and effect.

You make better choices if you know yourself well. Values and passion play a big part in this. In lots of ways we are imperfect beings in an imperfect world, trying to find as much perfection as we are able. Just always do your best. That's all that's ever expected of you.

Live each new day with great anticipation, look for the opportunities, and develop yourself spiritually. A deeper understanding of life will give you more inner power and will lead you to the purpose of your being. Life is so satisfying then. You will find that is the way to wisdom. Everything is created through your actions and by your thoughts. Feel in charge; change what isn't working and know that through discipline you can achieve all your desires. Just believe and get to know yourself and make all your choices around everything that is important to you.

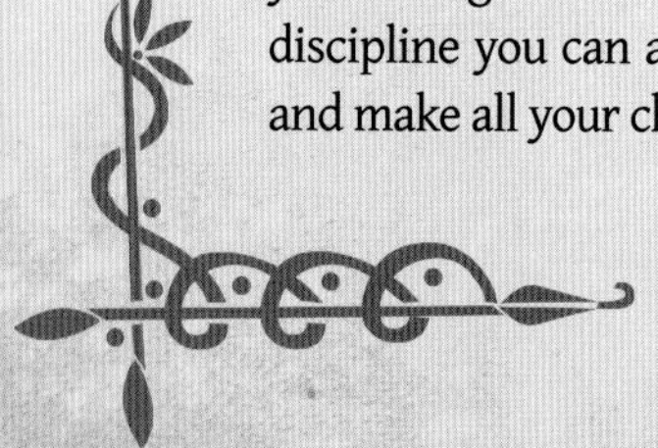

When you plant a red rose seed
you want to end up with a red rose to look at
or in your hand.
You are in charge;
never give your own power away
in your OWN Best Life.
There is no room for excuses –
why you can't do
what you want to do.
You are the limitation,
nobody else –
guaranteed.

Smile

page 92

A smile costs nothing but gives much.
It enriches those who receive, without making poorer those who give.
It takes but a moment, but the memory of it sometimes lasts forever.
None is so rich or mighty, that he can get along without it
and none is so poor but that he can be made rich by it.

A smile creates happiness in the home, fosters goodwill in business
and is the countersign of friendship.
It brings rest to the weary, cheer to the discouraged,
sunshine to the sad and it is nature's best antidote for trouble.

Yet it cannot be bought, begged, borrowed or stolen for it is
something that is of no value to anyone, until it is given away.
Some people are too tired to give you a smile.
Give them yours, as none needs a smile so much
as he who has no more to give.

Author Unknown

Notes

Chapter 12

The magic flow of life

Each day we must live our best life. We can do this by letting ourselves be directed by the flow of life. We must let our day support us. Whatever the day brings we need to go with it, even if it doesn't work out with all our plans, appointments and goals for that day. You will get the best result if you can be adaptable, just follow the direction of the day. Each day has a certain energy that changes all the time. Just work on keeping harmony in your day.

All you need is to have faith in life; it will always work out and you will also discover it supports you and gives you rewards. Mostly we don't gain much by forcing circumstances. This might not always be easy. I'm sure all of us make mistakes and do things we are not so proud of. Anger causes distance and upsetting interactions with others. Have you ever discovered that a person's distance could have been brought on by your anger and produced a consequence you didn't want? Forgive yourself first, learn, and set yourself up better next time. You are held responsible for your thoughts, actions and intentions. You are never superior to another human being. If we approach life this way we create self-esteem and we realise we are worthy and deserve the best. This way we open doors to a new and better future for ourselves. We always receive from others what we give to others.

It is helpful and interesting to see ourselves through the eyes of others. What do they think of me? What strength, weakness or potential do they think I have? To find out we could ask some people we admire or are friends with. The forthcoming information we could use in our daily life with others. If we let the day support us we give the universe a chance to make our dreams come true. Only by going with the flow can we achieve our goals. All other ways are hard work and often give poor results. The flow can take us out of our comfort zone, but that is the universe extending us, making our life bigger. We always have a choice to accept this or to stick to the familiar. In the end only we are responsible for our own actions. However if you want to achieve and look back at a well-lived life you must go after your dreams.

It also pays not to pay any attention to the obstacles that present themselves as we grow. The universe takes care and will solve everything in the way of your dreams. It will ask for a strong will, and if we focus on the problem they will grow bigger. However if we instead

concentrate our attention on finding solutions they will become visible to us. The magic flow of life takes care of that,if we just give it a chance. There is so much more to life than can be seen by the naked eye. We all have experiences with coincidences and out-of-the-blue happenings.

Believing in yourself, service to the human being, staying optimistic in this tight economic time, knowing you can do anything you put your mind to, and honouring the flow of life each and every day are the secrets of your best life. This doesn't mean that everything you do and say is right. It takes as much

courage to admit you are wrong. Always find your own peace of mind in everything that is important to you. This will create happiness. The magic flow of life will always support you.

Two years ago when I went to America for the Writer's Workshop for the publication of my book. I experienced a wonderful, interesting flow of life. In Miami I wanted to buy a particular book by Brian L. Weiss, who lives in this city. I thought this would be easy. The opposite was true. However it was my wish, so I kept trying – in vain. On the last evening, just before I flew away to go to see my family in Holland, I found the book I was looking for on a shelf in a bookshop I had been before. I had made enquiries and it was checked, but it didn't come up on the computer. The flow also created, that when I flew back home to see my family, using tickets I hadn't booked myself, I arrived on my birthday. I hadn't celebrated my birthday with my family for 33 years. Magic flow of life indeed.

An inspirational thought from Helen Steiner Rice:

Life is a highway
on which the years go by.
Sometimes the road is level,
sometimes the hills are high.

Finally go with the flow with small and big issues. Each day will show you how. Now and then taking some time out or just surrendering to the process will be very beneficial. Like me finding the book a day later in a shop I had already made inquiries in. There is always a time difference between asking and receiving. Whether by choice or circumstances, having a period to be alone to think and work things through can be very helpful. When we understand the right and wrong in situations and then identify what is best for us, we create flow, and the universe will support us in our quest for our wish. Always stay in charge of your OWN Best Life. Always go with how it feels to you – it must feel great to you; only that way can you create your own happiness. Nobody else can – guaranteed.

A return to love

page 99

Our deepest fear is not that we are inadequate.
Our deepest fear is that we are powerful beyond measure.
It is our light, not our darkness, that most frightens us.
We ask ourselves: "Who am I to be brilliant, gorgeous, talented, fabulous?"
Actually, who are you NOT to be?
You are a child of God.
Your playing small doesn't serve the world.
There's nothing enlightened about shrinking so that
other people won't feel insecure around you.
We are all meant to shine, as children do.
We were born to manifest the glory of God within us.
It's not just in some of us; it's in everyone.
And as we let our light shine, we consciously
give other people permission to do the same.
As we're liberated from our own fear,
our presence automatically liberates others.

Marianne Williamson

www.marianne.com

FAHEY
0800 343-996

The Arts Centre of

Notes

page 102

Chapter 13

The realisation of the beauty and difficulty of life

Just a few days ago I looked outside and there they were, some 50 small, beautifully coloured birds sitting in a long line on the top of my fence. What a sight. I just stopped and enjoyed this rarity. After a while they slowly flew away. They left me in awe, something not so easy to forget.

Life can touch us suddenly in unexpected and extraordinary ways. Nothing else seems important at that moment. We truly are in the now, in the natural flow of life. We all experience these moments and the secret lies in knowing it, to fully go with it.

We all experience difficult times in our life. Sometimes we are at a crossroad and must decide what is best for us at this time in our life. It could help to think, how important will this issue be for me in five years' time? The universe or infinite intelligence wants us to make our own choices and decisions in life. It will block our attempt to know our future path. Many options are always possible and it must always be up to the individual to decide what the best choice is at the time. You are the only one who can ever feel what is most important to you, so make sure you always decide to choose happiness.

The following poem from M. Scott Peck shows a very important way to understand and accept life. The first book that was lent to me and that I read on my journey of self-discovery was from this author – *The Road Less Travelled: The New Psychology of Love, Traditional Values and Spiritual Growth.* Soon afterwards I bought my own copy of this bestseller.

Life is difficult

page 105

This is a great truth,
one of the greatest truths.
It is a great truth because,
once we truly see this truth,
we transcend it.

Once we truly know that
life is difficult – once we truly
understand and accept it –
then life is no longer difficult.

Because once it is accepted,
the fact that life is difficult
no longer matters.

When we focus on solutions instead of the drama of our life we stay optimistic and hopeful. A major issue in my life over the last few years has been the writing and publication of this book. I had to have tenacity, determination, persistent effort, belief, creativity, enthusiasm, high expectations and finance, and be very disciplined about writing my book proposal and manuscript. The finished product is so satisfying to me. It confirms to me how important it is to work every day on your big goals.

Life easily takes over doing all the little things and obligations you are meant to do. It's also very interesting to notice that the advice I give to others comes back to my own self all the time. It helps to make me walk my talk. Unexpected outside circumstances also have major consequences. However nothing must discourage us from our big goal. Life will always test us. Our attitude is of vital importance. Delays are fine, but to never give up on your wish is to show what you made of. Winston Churchill is a good role model to keep in front of you in times of big challenges.

Stephen Covey is so right – our big goals come first in our daily life. All our other jobs, fun projects and duties have to fit in around our most important purpose. His demonstration shows clearly that if we don't put our big rocks (big goals) first into the jar, there will not be enough room left for all other stones, grit and water to fit in that same jar. Try it for yourself.

If you let life take over, the BIG GOALS will most likely never come to fruition.

How we feel is most important. So decide today to do all the things that make you feel the best.

To eat the food that make you feel the best.

To dress yourself in the clothes that make you feel the best.

To be with the people who make you feel the best.

To read the books that make you feel the best.

To watch the movies that make you feel the best.

To think the thoughts that make you feel the best.

The best will win every time!

Decide what is best for you!

Be the individual you want to be and you have all right to be.

Individuality

Have the courage to follow your own path

Have the courage to live

your OWN Best Life

A to Zen of life

Avoid negative sources, people, places and habits

Believe in yourself

Consider things from every angle

Don't give up and don't give in

Everything you're looking for lies behind the mask you wear

Family and friends are hidden treasures; seek them and enjoy their riches

Give more than you planned to

Hang on to your dreams

If opportunity doesn't knock, build a door

Judge your success by what you had to give up in order to get it

Keep trying no matter how hard it seems

Love yourself

Make it happen

Never lie, steal or cheat

Open your arms to change, but don't let go of your values

Practice makes perfect

Quality not quantity in anything you do

Remember that silence is sometimes the best answer

Stop procrastinating

Take control of your own destiny

Understand yourself in order to better understand others

Visualise it

When you lose, don't lose the lesson

Excellence in all your efforts

You are unique; nothing can replace you

Zero in on your target and go for it

Dalai Lama

Notes

page 110

Chapter 14

Time to make life easy

We all experience dark times in our life. We can't always control external events – an extreme example being the Christchurch earthquakes – but I like to think we certainly can control our own personal involvement. Mostly, however, when we decide on a different combination of actions we can bring about another result. Sometimes we need to give ourselves time to reflect on what is no longer beneficial in our lives.

We must take the learning from previous actions. As the saying goes, "you reap what you sow". Actions always have consequences. Once the choice is made it will affect your future. However it will benefit you when you can gracefully release those things life seeks to take away from you. For this to happen with ease we need to believe in ourselves. We need to know we are free and can decide what is right for us. We must not be stopped by limitations of mind and body. We form our future by the actions we take now. We must think about our lives, if we wish to understand it. We need to use our wisdom, which is the product of self-knowledge, and find a clear vision of our belief. Every experience has helped to form our character; our past is not just something that's happened. It's all an integral part of our choices, decisions and actions taken. We must therefore accept responsibility for ourselves.

When we go through darkness in our lives, we need faith and know that even in spite of the lack of evidence things can become better. Life does demand that you respond to every circumstance. Whatever we do and experience, it will always contribute to our personality. We realise that we must be careful in making any decisions, because we will have to live with the consequences of all our actions.

At all times I'm convinced that non-violent action is the answer to peace in your own life, your home and in our society. Every day the papers are full of violence, hurt, pain and loss of life.

I treat any act of violence – physical and/or emotional – with non-violence, with a passive resistance. This way I work towards a positive interaction, and in the end I believe it will benefit everyone involved. The hurt and grief of any type of violence never goes away, but the way you react will make a difference in your own recovery and it gives an example to our society as a whole. Treat all violence with love.

No matter what your wealth or power, we all know that old age, sickness and/or accidents will end your physical life – this counts for everyone. This truly makes us a leader in our own life.

We are the product of our decisions, not of our conditions. Sometimes it is important to balance the past with the future. This will take some self-examination, which entails forgiveness to the one who has hurt you and forgiveness to yourself for all your own mistakes. Always take charge and create a wonderful future for yourself.

Free yourself of the past; otherwise you will possibly keep repeating past behaviours with no satisfactory result in sight. When we do not truly know ourselves, we often follow certain patterns and this can lead us to act out of fear or guilt. You are always in charge, you have free will; there is no doubt about that. It just takes courage to use your free will. It is, however, important that your actions bring meaning and value to your life. No one can ever feel you, follow your heart, know what is right for you. When you look at your life, abandon all situations that give you low level satisfaction. Instead focus on what is more purposeful and lasting.

There are times when we must simplify our life. We may have too many appointments and obligations, too much work and not enough fun. Take a look this month at what changes you can make in your daily routine to simplify your life. I

have made some big decisions lately and have let go of some major commitments that stopped my enjoyment in life. I decided I needed to devote more of my time and energy to things that matter most to me. I do value my own opinion about myself. It takes confidence in oneself to pursue your main goals in life. I acknowledge it takes a great deal of self-love to believe in my own strengths and talents. I want to be free to decide what is right for me, without the need to follow the crowd or public opinion. I certainly don't want to feel oppressed; I want to use my free will and take charge of my future as I see fit. I want to grow and not stand still – life is to be lived to the full.

The learning from Tao Te Ching is that we are all great human beings. We come from greatness, we attract greatness and we are greatness. There's a pure, timeless energy that's within everything. We must understand the great within ourselves if we are to be able to attract this greatness of its own self to itself. This way we will meet the right people for our vision, and the perfect occasions we desire will take place. Life will become a very happy rollercoaster ride. It's our right to enjoy our life and have lots of fun on the way. Therefore decide today to claim your greatness, allow yourself to shine in whatever shape or form you do this. Tell yourself:

All is well in my world.

A time for everything

There is a time for everything,
and a season for every activity under heaven;
a time to be born and a time to die,
a time to plant and a time to uproot,
a time to kill and a time to heal,
a time to tear down and a time to build,
a time to weep and a time to laugh,
a time to mourn and a time to dance,
a time to scatter stones and a time to gather them,
a time to embrace and a time to refrain,
a time to search and a time to give up,
a time to keep and a time to throw away,
a time to tear and a time to mend,
a time to be silent and a time to speak,
a time to love and a time to hate,
a time for war and a time for peace.

Ecclesiastes 3;1-8

Time

Take time to think,
it is the source of power.
Take time to play,
it is the secret of perpetual life.
Take time to read,
it is the foundation of wisdom.
Take time to pray,
it is the greatest power on Earth.
Take time to love, and be loved,
it is a God-given privilege.
Take time to be friendly,
it is the road to happiness.
Take time to laugh,
it is the music of the soul.
Take time to give,
it is too short a day to be selfish.

Author unknown

Notes

page 118

Chapter 15

How important is financial independence in your life?

The journey to financial freedom starts when you decide that your destiny is abundant and will be prosperous. It's my intention to be financially independent in the future. I know this is a big ask in my life. It has been and still is a battle to take full charge of my material responsibilities. It needs my optimism and my belief that I can do it and that I'm worth it. I know that money opens doors, and when you have plenty of it you can do a lot of good in this world.

These last two years I have been greatly tested in my financial responsibilities. I needed quite a bit of money up front to realise my dream of publishing this book, yet my cash flow wasn't in a wonderful state. However to obtain an increase on my mortgage or a separate loan from the bank was never going to be an easy task. I'm single, with no security of income, living through earthquakes and natural uncertainty, plus there's a worldwide economic recession. Only a job could bring me a secure income, and then most likely the loan would be honoured and I would have raised the money for the publication of the book. The book would provide the improvement of my financial situation. Again a risky adventure – not in my eyes, but from the responsible bank manager's point of view certainly. I have no proven record of success.

The job I wanted would have to be as a coach, mentor or consultant because I wanted to provide a service, instead of going back to my old ways of number crunching. It is my wish now to put my time and energy to direct benefit of others. I decided to go with the flow, because I trust the flow knows where to go in a setback. I have experienced that it does. The book is proof.

Diana Cooper's book *2012 and Beyond*, says that in the future we will work towards living in a world without ego, power, struggle, personal drive or ambition. All we will look for is the wish to express ourselves creatively and serve others. This is a comfort to me, because that is where my strength lies. I have great capability in the intuition and emotional fields. She says this in return will create peace, joy and contentment. A perfect life – what else could we possibly ask for? There will be no money or banks, just an exchange of energy. People will produce what is necessary for their own needs and anything else will be freely exchanged. This is hard to put our head around at this stage of our life, considering how we experience the world as it is now. The universe is, however, working to bring us together, to teach us what our life is all about and what is important. There are many extreme happenings and changes taking place all over the globe. I lived through the Christchurch earthquakes of 4 September 2010, 22 February 2011, 13 June 2011 and 23 December 2011, plus their many aftershocks (after 500 days on 17th January 2012, we recorded 9500 quakes, magnitude 3+ and we are still counting) and I can say with great certainty that they have brought the community together. Our city is broken, but the people are coming together in unity to build a new place to be proud of. The thought of giving up never enters the mind.

It's interesting to mention that in numerology it is a fact that most earthquakes and great disasters happen on a 2 – 4 – 8 and 22 vibration. The universal year 2011 has a 4 vibration. All the major quakes in Christchurch happened on a 4 and 8 vibration, except the 23rd December 2011 – a 5 vibration.

A few years ago I went to a seminar for coaching. There was a speaker at this conference who taught us that everything that's happening is in our mind-set. After his speech we had to write down what stood out most for us from his talk. I wrote that I have a millionaire's mind-set. He made me stand up, shake his hand and promise me I would become a millionaire. I made the promise in front of a hall full of people. At the time I was reading a book called *How to Have a Millionaire's Mindset* by Pat Mesiti. It was in my handbag. I drive a car with a bright standard yellow

LIFE COACH & NUMEROLOGIST

BSTLFE

BESTLIFE.CO.NZ

sign, "Future millionaire on board". In my house I have a framed $1,000,000.00 play banknote (looks real) hanging on the wall above my desk in my bedroom. I have a certificate with my name on it from One Minute Millionaire that says I hereby decide to become an Enlightened Millionaire so I can eliminate my money pressures, enjoy a life of complete financial freedom, and share my abundance with others, signed fifteenth day of October 2006 by Robert & Allen, co- author, The One Minute Millionaire.

I do believe strongly that we need to surrender to life, not force any issues around money. This will open up choices and options you would never have thought of before. Watch closely for any opportunities, face your fears and create new possibilities. That way you will be ready to receive all that you are meant to have – guaranteed.

Remember

Remember life is a journey
and you are not alone.

Remember no matter what happens
there is sunshine after rain.

Remember your work is part of your life
not all of your life.

Remember every problem has a solution
and you can only do your best.

Remember when you start believing in yourself
the sky is the limit.

Remember what stops you from succeeding is you.

Remember it's your life
and you have the choice to make a difference.

In the end it's up to you.

Author unknown

Notes

Chapter 16

The end of the year is near

The end of the year is near. I think it is always very helpful to look back at the year and see how it all went. Are you happy with the result? Has Numerology guided you and did it all make sense? Each Personal Year has its own characteristics, and as you look at each month and day's influence you will become aware of more detail again. Never forget the universal vibration.

We are complicated human beings. Relationships play vital roles in our life. Everybody works with their own vibrations, and other people's can be quite different from your own at that time. Understanding yourself and others is important for a successful life.

Each year we deal with different vibrations and as we understand the reasons for these differences, year after year, we start to come to terms with ourselves and the people in our lives.

Understanding will give clarity and take the stress and challenge out of life. It teaches you to never take anything personal; people do the things they are drawn to – these are not real, just a passing stage.

The life you currently live is the result of all your past thoughts and actions. This month look back at your life and decide what you want to do, be and have. If you don't like something think of some changes you could make such as to your responses – negative to positive thoughts, habits, what you read, your friends or the way you talk.

If you have been affected by an abnormal event or personal loss of some kind in the year be very kind to yourself. When we experience trauma we always feel this in a very personal way. We have our own individual reaction to the event or loss, such as being in a state of shock, fear, disbelief, irritability, anxiety, sadness, grief, helplessness or numbness. We may experience sleep disturbances, crying, tearfulness, hyper-vigilance or withdrawal from others, and we may increase our intake of alcohol or drugs. Our physical symptoms can be expressed through having feelings of hot or cold sensations, dizziness, nervousness, exhaustion, headaches, nausea, amd tightness in the throat and chest. There may also be confusion, disorientation, repeated flashbacks, poor concentration and memory problems. We must realise this is all normal. We must allow ourselves time to heal. There are lots of ways to help ourselves. This is also very individual. You would know what is best for you based on how it feels to you. The road to finding happiness again is a process, a winding road.

Ways to make you feel better are by creating time for yourself to rest, or to talk to friends, and also often by not being alone. Always try to maintain as normal a schedule as possible – sleep, breakfast, lunch, dinner and some exercise. Your feelings are important, so make a point of expressing them. Stay in contact with family and friends.

By contrast, if you know people who experienced an extraordinary event or personal loss during the year try to spend some time with them and listen to their stories. Always make them feel safe, maybe help them out with ordinary household duties or minding the children. Express how sorry you feel about their experience or loss. Just try to understand and assist them.

Life can bring us some unexpected, difficult experiences. Over the last one and a half years we have experienced many changes in Christchurch through major earthquakes and many, many aftershocks. Our ground is unstable, which causes anxiety among people. We become unsure about life. We hear stories and people trying to predict and explain what is happening. I believe it is important you find your own inner calm. You can do this through deep breathing, meditation, listening to soothing music, watching a comedy or going for a walk in a natural environment. Try not to put any attention to all the negative predictions; instead put all your attention to today. It must be your intention to make it your very best day and decide to be happy and optimistic about life. Stay in your own power – don't give it away to anyone.

We can't avoid death – it brings rebirth. Christchurch is a broken city but it will live again, more beautiful than before. The people living in this city must stay positive, and together we will build again. It will be a privilege to be part of the process. We will feel proud and leave a legacy for many generations to enjoy after us.

Life will always bring challenges. Life is never staying the same. When we are on top of the world, living on cloud nine, life will change. Never ever can we hang on to great happiness or deep sorrow.

Life has its highs and lows, like the sea has high and low tide. When we live through our nine-year cycle, some years our tide is high, other years low – and in year nine we deal with both tides. Years 2-11/2-4-6 are low and year 7 even slower; years 1-3-22/4-5 are high and year 8 even faster.

When the tide is high we can achieve a lot in our life whereas when the tide is low our opportunities and accomplishments are limited. In low years we need to show much more patience. Our personal lives and the universe will always change and will go through the tides.

An ancient Chinese story shows this well:

An old man had one son, one horse and a small farm on the edge of a village. One day his horse broke free and ran away. The villagers gathered together and visited the old man to tell him how sorry they were about his bad luck.

"Bad luck? How do you know it is bad luck? It might be a blessing," he said. The villagers were a little confused as they left.

Several weeks later the horse returned, along with a herd of wild horses. The farmer now had 14 horses. The villagers gathered together and visited him to tell him how lucky he was.

"Lucky? How do you know it is good fortune? It might be a problem," he said.

One week later, his son fell from one of the wild horses and was trampled, severely injuring his legs. He became crippled for life. Once again the villagers visited to offer their condolences.

"Unfortunate? How do you know this? It might be a blessing," the old man replied.

Late in the following year the Emperor declared war on a neighbouring country, and all the able-bodied men were summoned to fight. The old man's son was unable to go as he was maimed. The war lasted two seasons, during which time all the men from the village who had fought died. Once again the villagers visited to tell the old man how lucky he was.

"Lucky? How do you know that this is fortunate? It might be a problem."

Life changes and it always will. Why does it change? Nobody really knows. Most likely we need to learn and evolve when we are in this physical form and living our lives. The most important is that you realise you are always in charge. You can always decide how you will react to the change.

Will you decide to go with the flow, meet the opportunities as they present themselves to you, or will you built a wall and feel out of control? Stay positive and life will deal you positive cards. You attract what you think and feel. Focus on solutions and they will become clear to you. Try not to stay in the drama of life; go forward. We can never change yesterday. We live today and have our hopes for tomorrow.

Always let Numerology help you. You will not be disappointed. I guarantee you. Maybe you're looking for a gift with a difference for a birthday or Christmas for a very special person. Decide to buy this personal, self-empowering book – *Best of Life.*

Life is a journey

We are all passengers

On a boat called

Life

And we are all alive

In the moment called

Now

The journey of life is so beautiful

That it needs no destination

Author unknown

17

Notes

page 132

Chapter 17

The twelve gifts I wish for everyone

It's hard to believe, but the last month of this year is upon us. Time is always the same, yet still somehow I find the years seem to go by faster. I wonder if this is because we live such full lives or that energy is spinning faster.

According to numerology we are all preparing for a new Personal Year, and at the same time it's also of great importance to look back on this year and reflect how far you have come.

Are you satisfied with your results and input of this year?

Have you spent your own time and energy well?

Has Numerology helped you in your best direction for this year, month and day?

I would like to finish the year with giving you twelve gifts to think of and reflect upon:

1. Be optimistic and you will notice that life will turn out all right.
2. Be passionate and do what you love in life.
3. Play, laugh, have fun and enjoy yourself.
4. Be the master of your own time and energy.
5. Take risks – the greater the risk, the greater your potential for success in life.
6. Love unconditionally and love for ever, but mostly love yourself.
7. Take time to read a book; knowledge gets you far in life.
8. Be action orientated, and results will follow.
9. Be healthy – nurture yourself from the inside out.
10. Your thoughts create your life; change your thoughts and that will change your life.
11. Family and friends: treasure special memories of the past and today.
12. Happiness: you will find your happiness deep down within.

The greatest gift to yourself is to know yourself, to love yourself, to understand your purpose in this life, and to have lots of fun. We are always in charge of our lives, even if we think we aren't. Everything has a reason. We learn and we always have a choice to make it better. We are not perfect human beings. We make many mistakes. I don't know anybody who isn't flawed somewhere. We are all on a journey. Try to accept yourself as you are – be kind to yourself. Even when you struggle with addictions of any kind, depression, being overweight or being unemployed. Find a way to accept yourself – to just love yourself with all the imperfections that you know are part of you.

This month be generous to yourself and you will find that the things you most desire will just happen. Let the feeling go of you not being worthy of love, success, fun and abundance. The reason why we find it difficult at times to go forward is our fear of being humiliated. We all have been humiliated at times in our lives. Often we remember these times vividly. We identify them as our worst nightmare but we've all had to live through such nightmares and make them part of our experience. They have helped us to grow and made us a human being.

We all have a fear of failing. When we make use of our common sense and our understanding of others, then we will deal with these issues in our lives the best. I suggest for the last month of the year you create some joy in your life, and with that a plan of action. Let Christmas be a happy time for you, irrelevant of your circumstances.

Start with looking after yourself – you have no control over the external world. Your best guidance is your intuitive knowing, your instinct. Your own conscience will help you to choose to be good, generous, kind and honest.

With your plan of action find your highest potential and take charge of your own happiness. It is a process, a beautiful journey. Your life is yours, so live up to your very best. Expect your own input; don't depend on others to create joy in your life. The twelve gifts can be a focus and a help if you use them on the twelve days before Christmas.

Last but not least, MERRY CHRISTMAS to all of you.

You are unique

since everybody is an individual

nobody can be you

you are unique

no one can tell you how to use your time

it is yours

your life is your own

you mould it

you make it

Remember

always that

you have not

only the right to

be an individual,

you have an

obligation

to be one.

Eleanor Roosevelt

Notes

page 138

page 139

Section Two

Numerology

Chapter 18

History of numerology

Living our OWN Best Life is the most important issue in our precious life. To do this we need to know ourselves really well. Then we will realise that we live our life in cycles and that history can repeat itself. I truly believe in the science of numbers: Numerology can help you greatly with living your life well and also with understanding other human beings in your life. So why do I think this?

I'm sure if I had known this science earlier in my own life I would have made different choices at certain times. I'm also confident I would have been better in charge of my own time and energy at all times. Numerology gives answers on questions like, What is my purpose? What is my destiny? What am I to achieve? What will make me happy? What am I naturally good at?

Let's start from the beginning. Numerology is not new, not a trend, not psychic, not fortune-telling, not clairvoyance. Numerology is the science of numbers and goes back at least 2500 years. Since the start of human history, numbers have been a source of information and understanding of people and the world around us. The ancient Chaldeans, Egyptians, Assyrians, Babylonians, Greeks, Hindus and Hebrews all developed numerological systems of their own, and to this day Numerology is constantly being updated and expanded by various experts and cultures. The Pythagoreans provided a method of interpreting numbers by the qualities assigned to them, known as the Pythagorean Philosophy of Numbers based upon the "Laws of Opposites", discussed in next chapter. Pythagoras, a Greek mathematician who lived about five centuries BC, never wrote a book and any fragmentary records of his students were purposely destroyed so they wouldn't fall into the hands of those who would misuse their wisdom. However a scientific system is evidenced by fragments of his teachings that have been left to the world.

Pythagoras believed that numbers are the foundation of the universe, that the world is built on the power of numbers. This is why the numbers 1-9 are the basis of all numbers and calculations in Numerology. The same reduction can take place with words and letters.

In the beginning of the 20th century this science came to the attention of Mrs L. Dow Balliett of Atlantic City, in America. She was a music teacher and specialised in musical composition. She is recognised as the founder of the Balliett Philosophy of

Number Vibration. She wrote several books about the vibration of letters and music, which she called "number vibration". She said a person's Life Song in musical notes is found by using the digits of the month, day and year of birth. She rearranged the musical chart, making C the first note instead of A (six note). According to her everything has three parts: that of Body, Soul and Spirit. The two silent parts, the Soul and Spirit, are dependent for expression upon the third part, which is the Body, and the audible expression of 1 (C note) and 2 (D note). She could not make it scientific, unless she used the fundamental C for the one, allowing the two previous silent notes to find expression through the audible one which expresses Trinity of 1 (C note), 2 (D note) and 3 (E note). This way the System is as scientific as is music. The master numbers 11 (C note) and 22 (D note) are high notes, the number 8 (C note) and 9 (D note) are either middle or high notes. The table is as follows:

C	D	E	F	G	A	B
1	2	3	4	5	6	7
8	9					
11	22					

It was a significant discovery to realise, that the letter name of a musical note and its sound have the same vibration.

Among Balliett's students were Florence Campbell (who wrote Your Days are Numbered), Dr. Julia Seton – founder of the New Thought Church and School (Church of the New Civilisation) – and her daughter, Dr. Juno Jordan. Dr. Seton gave the science the new name "Numerology" and helped through her lectures to make the science well known in the world. Her daughter carried on her work, writing several books of which Numerology, the Romance in your Name is the most well-known. She founded the Institute of Numerical Research, incorporated in the State of California. The association gave them the right and privilege to teach and counsel, as well as legal protection and professional standing. The purpose was to prove or disprove numerology and the influence of numbers in the human experience. For twenty-five years they took up for examination every phase of analysis they had ever heard of. Each member examined and tested each idea and reported his/her findings, until together they proved and proved beyond a doubt, that NUMBERS ARE SYMBOLS OF THOUGHT, ACTION, EXPERIENCE, HUMAN PURPOSE AND DIVINE PROPHECY. They are unfailing in their purpose and direction. It is only because we, with limited understanding of their direction and influence, sometimes fail to interpret their true meaning, that they seem to be untrue. Our names are life's love stories. The institute was closed by its founder and members after they were assured, that their analysis and methods were accurate.

Everything in this universe vibrates, and to be able to measure and explain this energy we need numbers. Numerology is the science of numbers; it is the key to all mysteries because only through numbers can we explain the vibrational content of any and all things.

There are two generally recognised methods of converting letters into numerical values.

The first and certainly oldest method comes from the Chaldean and Hebrew alphabet of numbering. Each letter is assigned to a number based on the sound of the letter. Those with similar vocal sounds are grouped together.

1	**2**	**3**	**4**	**5**	**6**	**7**	**8**
A	B	C	D	E	U	O	F
I	K	G	M	H	V	Z	P
J	R	L	T	N	W		
Q		S		X			
Y							

There is no number nine because it was the number of finality in Hebrew mythology. The number nine is believed to have sacred significance. Nothing could ever be truly final in the Hebrew philosophy and they had no letter sounds which could convey the concept of finality or totality. Only one thing could ever be perfect and complete – their God.

The second method, the Pythagorean system, uses is a more modern approach:

1	**2**	**3**	**4**	**5**	**6**	**7**	**8**	**9**
A	B	C	D	E	F	G	H	I
J10/1	K11/2	L12/3	M13/4	N14/5	O15/6	P16/7	Q17/8	R18/9
S19/1	T20/2	U21/3	V22/4	W23/5	X24/6	Y25/7	Z26/8	

Both systems can be used with equal success. The Pythagorean system is more widely used.

In Numerology we will always reduce names and dates from their double digit numbers to single ones, the exceptions being 11 and 22, the master numbers, which vibrate higher, causing number 11 to be called a "spiritual messenger" and 22 is considered the "spiritual master in form".

Each of the numbers has its own values and characteristics. The numbers will never lie; however the interpretation can be wrong because of our limited understanding of their direction and influence. The science of Numerology will always need research and is limitless. I'm every time astonished how true the information is. As much as we can explain people, so we can also include our pets, our home, business, city, country, colours, flowers – actually everything around us. For as long as we live on this planet the numbers are symbols of thought, action, experience, human purpose and divine prophecy. Numerology helps you to explain your energy in a grounded, analytical and scientific way.

Numerology is a character analysis. Our date of birth and our name at birth are an autobiography of our life. Numerology is a guide and this book focuses on your date of birth; using this we can find your personal year, month and day, and your lucky day. This information will give you a clear direction about when it is the best time to execute your plans and ideas. My next book will focus on our name.

For as long as human beings have lived there has been a wish to know the future. For us to know the future we have to look at the past. Numerology can help and shows you that your life has a way of repeating itself. This will help you to be more in charge of your life and able to change outcomes if you don't like what is happening. It is of great importance that you remember the significant events in your life and what year they took place. It can be difficult to remember the complete past; sometimes our memories fail us to bring back the exact years when important experiences took place. But once we have all this data the future will be easier to embrace and control. Knowing the past is the key to your future. Start writing the significant dates of events in your life in this book. It will help you greatly in establishing the re-occurring experiences in your life.

The first and best step to take is for you to look back at your life nine and eighteen years ago. You are now today in the process of living through similar energy to these past times. It is important to know how you coped then and what you can do now for a better or similar result. You are in charge of your life and choices at all times. By remembering the past you can definitely get an insight in to what is most likely to happen in the future. History has a remarkable way of repeating itself. What we are destined to come across in life will happen, but we are in charge how we are going to face up and deal with our destiny.

Fate seems to repeat itself. We most likely get tested again on similar issues. We will deal with it differently each time – for instance, suffer less or more. We must hope to grow wiser with age and we achieve this through intelligence. The seedling will grow over time, it will not mature as soon as it is planted.

Whatever happens in our life has a purpose, and always you are the only one responsible for your own actions at all times. Nobody can ever tell you what is the right thing to do at this moment in time, but you can work out your best action by how it feels to you. You know for certain what feels good. You will get punished for the wrong choices in your life. Today you can make the choice to create the change you are looking for.

Always stay in your own power; you will always know best. Look for the patterns in your life. Find the critical points. We can learn from past happenings, gaining strength from seeing how we survived, and this will help us reclaim ourselves more quickly in the present day.

Every time you remember a significant event write the age you were and if it was a positive or a negative experience. Remember you are always in charge now of your choices. You can turn the table if you are looking for better results in your life. You must take control of your existence and prepare yourself to make better choices that will create happiness and good fortune in your future.

As we grow older we learn from experiences and can get insight how we react with similar issues in our life. After the age of 36 (four 9-year periods) we most likely understand ourselves better and start to see how we react to certain repeated situations in our life. Of great importance is to see the positive and the negative flows in the cycle. You must break destructive cycles or fate for better results and thereby create your OWN Best Life.

Whatever personal year, month and day (Chapters 20, 21 and 22) you are in now, you will have experienced similar episodes nine and eighteen years ago. We can never forget the universal vibration, which is always around us and has a significant impact on our lives. We must always understand and integrate both our personal and universal vibration. As an example in Christchurch the universal energy, which caused the natural disaster has a great impact on your daily, monthly and yearly life. However we make our own lives, decide our own choices and if we live on the positive side of our own personal vibration, we can live our own very Best Life and have everything we possible want.

Each year decide to write a few lines in this book about what has happened in your life. This way you will easily remember all major occasions in your life. It will benefit you many times over, when you look back at your life and see what you can expect and how you can prepare yourself for the choices you always have in the now.

Life truly is amazing
and precious,
and numerology
can help you to make sense of it all
guaranteed.

Notes

page 150

Some interesting analysis about numbers

Twin towers and the number eleven

Why was the attack on the Twin Towers on 11th September?

It is interesting to see how Numerology explains this well-known historical event.

New York City has 11 letters

New York City was the 11th state added to the Union.

Afghanistan has 11 letters

The Pentagon has 11 letters

The date of the attack is 11 September known as 9/11: 9+1+1 =11

September 11th is the 254th day of the year: 2+5+4=11

The total number of victims inside all the planes was 254

The Twin Towers standing side by side looked like number 11

The first plane to hit the towers was Flight 11

Flight 11 had 92 people on board 9+2=11

Flight 77 had 65 people on board 6+5=11

The emergency number in America is telephone number 911: 9+1+1=11

The most recognised symbol for the US, after the Stars & Stripes, is the Eagle.

The following verse is taken from the Koran, the Islamic holy book:

"For it is written that a son of Arabia would awaken a fearsome Eagle. The wrath of the Eagle would be felt throughout the lands of Allah. While some of the people trembled in despair still more rejoiced: for the wrath of the Eagle cleansed the lands of Allah and there was peace."

That verse is number 9.11 of the Koran.

Highlight the Q33 NY. This is the flight number of a plane to hit one of the Twin Towers.

Change the font on your computer to WINGDINGS, this is what you will see:

The union of the Fire triangle and the Water triangle is shown through interlaced triangles.

If we look at the meaning of twin it is each of a closely related or associated pair, it is a link or cause (a town) to link with one in a different country, for the purposes of friendship and cultural exchange. The number eleven adds up to the number two. The number two symbol is 2, ii, ll. The two is one more than one; the sum of one unit and another unit such as two people, two groups of people, two towns, two countries etc. By putting two and two together, we have two towers and two groups of people. We could divide the two groups of people in the aware and the unaware, the sane and the insane, the good and the bad. It is very sad indeed, that in this event the link wasn't for the purpose of friendship and cultural exchange.

Magic squares

There are seven magic squares, each dedicated to a planet. Maybe one is holding your winning numbers; try looking at the number of the day you were born on (birth number) in the various squares diagonally, horizontally and vertically.

In the Square of Saturn has nine individual numbers in three columns and the sum of each line is 15 and the sum of all numbers in the square is 45. All squares can be added vertically, horizontally and diagonally with the same total always.

4	9	2
3	5	7
8	1	6

The Square of Jupiter has sixteen individual numbers in four columns and the sum of each line is 34 and the sum of all numbers in the square is 136. All squares can be added vertically, horizontally and diagonally with the same total always.

4	14	15	1
9	7	6	12
5	11	10	8
16	2	3	13

The Square of Mars has twenty-five individual numbers in five columns and the sum of each line is 65 and the sum of all numbers in the aquare is 325. All squares can be added vertically, horizontally and diagonally with the same total always.

11	24	7	20	3
4	12	25	8	16
17	5	13	21	9
10	18	1	14	22
23	6	19	2	15

The Square of the Sun has thirty-six numbers in six columns and the sum of each line is 111 and the sum of all numbers in the square is 666. All squares can be added vertically, horizontally and diagonally with the same total always.

6	32	3	34	35	1
7	11	27	28	8	30
19	14	16	15	23	24
18	20	22	21	17	13
25	29	10	9	26	12
36	5	33	4	2	31

The Square of Venus is forty-nine numbers in seven columns and the sum of each line is 175 and the sum of all numbers in the square is 1225. All squares can be added vertically, horizontally and diagonally with the same total always.

22	47	16	41	10	35	4
5	23	48	17	42	11	29
30	6	24	49	18	36	12
13	31	7	25	43	19	37
38	14	32	1	26	44	20
21	39	8	33	2	27	45
46	15	40	9	34	3	28

The Square of Mercury is sixty-four numbers in eight columns and the sum of each line is 260 and the sum of all numbers in the square is 2,080. All squares can be added vertically, horizontally and diagonally with the same total always.

8	58	59	5	4	62	63	1
49	15	14	52	53	11	10	56
41	23	22	44	45	19	18	48
32	34	35	29	28	38	39	25
40	26	27	37	36	30	31	33
17	47	46	20	21	43	42	24
9	55	54	12	13	51	50	16
64	2	3	61	60	6	7	57

The Square of the Moon is eighty-one numbers in nine columns and the sum of each line is 369 and the sum of all numbers in the square is 3,321. All squares can be added vertically, horizontally and diagonally with the same total always.

37	78	29	70	21	62	13	54	5
6	38	79	30	71	22	63	14	46
47	7	39	80	31	72	23	55	15
16	48	8	40	81	32	64	24	56
57	17	49	9	41	73	33	65	25
26	58	18	50	1	42	74	34	66
67	27	59	10	51	2	43	75	35
36	68	19	60	11	52	3	44	76
77	28	69	20	61	12	53	4	45

Love number six

Number six is the first perfect number, as originally divined by Euclid.

This is in when the factors of the number (numbers which divide into it) add up to the number itself.

The segments of six are 1, 2 and 3, 1 + 2 + 3 = 6 and 1 x 2 x 3 = 6

The number six is divisible by both an odd number three and an even number two thus harmoniously combining the elements of each.

God created all things in six days.

The sixth hour was the hour that Christ died on the cross.

The sixth Commandment: Thou shalt not kill.

Intuitive numbers seven and nine

The numbers seven and nine are both very special and somehow related as well.

Number seven is the only number that divides and repeats its number regardless of how many zeros you have after the one. 1,000,000 / 7 = 142,857 repeated.

This number makes a connection with number nine by multiplying with seven: 142,857 x 7=999,999

It is also called a famous puzzle number, because it seems to produce the same digits rearranged up till the perfect number six:

142,857 x 1 = 142,857

142,857 x 2 = 285,714

142,857 x 3 = 428,571

142,857 x 4 = 571,428

142,857 x 5 = 714,285

142,857 x 6 = 857,142

The number seven is known for:

Seven generations from David to the birth of Jesus Christ.

Seven days of creation, which is our week.

Seven creative planets of mankind – the Sun, Moon, Jupiter, Mercury, Venus, Saturn and Mars.

Later two more planets were discovered – Uranus in 1781 and Neptune in 1846 – that rule the mental and spiritual side of life and much later on 12th March 1930 the planet Pluto was discovered. First it was thought to be another planet, but it is smaller than our own moon, smaller than some of the satellites of the giant planets, and it is not the only body moving in the far reaches of the Solar System. In fact there is a whole swarm of them. I quote the astronomer Sir Patrick Moore from his book *Countdown! Or how nigh is the end?* The planets Uranus and Neptune awaken extra sensory perception and bring man into contact with the invisible side of life. Pluto carries this one step further. Since 1930 interest in metaphysics and occultism is more widespread than ever before. There has been scientific research into intuition and extrasensory perception (ESP), which includes clairvoyance, clairaudience, psychometry and mental telepathy. Hypnotism is being used by doctors and psychiatrist.

Seven primary harmonious musical notes, which are the basis of all music.

Seven chakra centres in our human body are at the base of the spine, lower abdomen, solar plexus, heart, throat, third eye and crown.

Each energy centre bears a different colour. The order of the colours run from the base of the spine to the top of the head (called the crown), the same as the Tree of Life, and run as follows: red, orange, yellow, green, blue, indigo and violet.

Seven colours in the rainbow, the same as from the energy centres, except in the rainbow red appears at the top and violet at the bottom. They are the basis of all combinations of colours.

The number nine is the only number that represents all and also continually returns.

For example: any number times nine returns to nine: 9 x 7 = 63 and 6 + 3 = 9

Any number added to or subtracted from nine returns to itself:

$$6 + 9 = 15 \text{ and } 1 + 5 = 6$$

$$35 - 9 = 26 \text{ and } 2 + 6 = 8$$

Add all single numbers 1+2+3+4+5+6+7+8+9 together and you get 45, which adds up to 9.

A complete circle is 360 degrees, which adds up to 9.

Nine is used to express ourselves – I want the whole nine yards, I'm on cloud nine, I'm dressed up to the nines, and nine times out of ten.

The number nine is the highest single number, which represents a whole cycle, a full nine-Personal-Year period. It is interesting to compare this to the nine months a mother will carry her baby, which represents an ending of pregnancy and the start of a new life and new beginning.

Finally there are many fascinating patterns associated with nine. For instance, write the digits 0 through 9 vertically and write the same sequence upwards. The result is the multiplication table for 9 – each pair of digits sums up to 9.

Then look at these patterns:

$$0 \times 9 + 1 = 1$$

$$1 \times 9 + 2 = 11$$

$$12 \times 9 + 3 = 111$$

$$123 \times 9 + 4 = 1{,}111$$

$$1234 \times 9 + 5 = 11{,}111$$

$$12345 \times 9 + 6 = 111{,}111$$

$$123456 \times 9 + 7 = 1{,}111{,}111$$

$$1234567 \times 9 + 8 = 11{,}111{,}111$$

$$12345678 \times 9 + 9 = 111{,}111{,}111$$

$$123456789 \times 9 + 10 = 1{,}111{,}111{,}111 \text{ etc.}$$

$$12{,}345{,}679 \times 9 = 111{,}111{,}111$$

$$12{,}345{,}679 \times 18 = 222{,}222{,}222$$

$$12{,}345{,}679 \times 27 = 333{,}333{,}333$$

$$12{,}345{,}679 \times 36 = 444{,}444{,}444$$

$$12{,}345{,}679 \times 45 = 555{,}555{,}555$$

$$12{,}345{,}679 \times 54 = 666{,}666{,}666$$

$$12{,}345{,}679 \times 63 = 777{,}777{,}777$$

$$12{,}345{,}679 \times 72 = 888{,}888{,}888$$

$$12{,}345{,}679 \times 81 = 999{,}999{,}999$$

and to top it off:

$$12{,}345{,}679 \times 999{,}999{,}999 = 12{,}345{,}678{,}987{,}654{,}321$$

Desiderata

Go placidly amidst the noise and haste, and remember what peace there may be in silence.

As far as possible without surrender be on good terms with all persons.

Speak your truth quietly and clearly; and listen to others, even the dull and ignorant;

they too have their story.

Avoid loud and aggressive persons; they are vexatious to the spirit.

If you compare yourself with others, you may become bitter or vain, for always there will be greater and lesser persons than yourself.

Enjoy your achievements as well as your plans.

Keep interested in your own career, however humble,

it is a real possession in the changing fortunes of time.

Exercise caution in your business affairs; for the world is full of trickery.

But let this not blind you to what virtue is; many persons strive for high ideals;

and everywhere life is full of heroism.

Be yourself.

Especially, do not feign affection.

Neither be cynical about love;

for in the face of all aridity and disenchantment it is perennial as the grass.

Take kindly the counsel of the years, gracefully surrendering the things of youth.

Nurture strength of spirit to shield you in sudden misfortune.

But do not distress yourself with imaginings.

Many tears are born of fatigue and loneliness.

Beyond a wholesome discipline, be gentle with yourself.

You are a child of the Universe, no less than the trees and the stars; you have a right to be here.

And whether or not it is clear to you, no doubt the universe is unfolding as it should.

Therefore be at peace with God, whatever you conceive Him to be, and whatever your labours and aspirations in the noisy confusion of life keep peace with your soul.

With all its sham, drudgery and broken dreams, it is still a beautiful world.

Be cheerful.

Strive to be happy.

Max Ehrmann

Notes

page 166

page 167

Chapter 19

Characteristics numbers 1-9 and master numbers 11 and 22

Number one

Positive: powerful, independent, original, dominant, executive ability, self-determination, active.

Negative: intolerant, egotistical, aggressive, boastful, greedy, prideful, obsessed.

Symbol: the Sun. Positive aspect: Zodiac sign of Leo 21st July- 20th August.

This number is introvert.

Weekday: Sunday.

The first number stands for creation, beginnings. Everything starts with the ones – new ways of doing things. They are the pioneers, powerful people, leaders. They have tenacity, self-assertiveness and show courage with their convictions. They are creative, build their own individuality, are courageous, determined and have strong views. This number stands for action, for standing on its own feet, to be independent. Continually adjusts itself to new situations. Time to start new projects and let the past behind.

The negative aspect of this number would be seen by individuals who could do higher work in life if they just could become more aware of their inner selves. People who have always been dependent on others and haven't or maybe couldn't or never had an opportunity in life to be assertive or self-reliant.

Number two

Positive: emotional, receptive, understanding, balance, partnership, diplomacy, sensitivity, tact.

Negative: Cruel, deceitful, self-conscious, alone, timid, scheming, meddling.

Symbol: the Moon. Positive aspect: Zodiac sign of Cancer, 21st June- 20th July.

This number is extrovert.

Weekday: Monday.

The number two is gentle by nature, imaginative, artistic and romantic. They are calm and like beauty. They bring all kinds of individuals and conditions together. They will avoid arguments, instead look for cooperation. They are the peacemakers and reflective. They harmonise and are diplomatic and tactful. They take responsibility for the finest, smallest detail, work with small objects, instruments and collect. They want to be with other people; they work well in groups, with friends, family or the community. Relationships are important. They stay always in the background.

The negative aspect of this number would be seen by individuals who are indecisive, feel often discontent with life, have very few opinions themselves and are easily persuaded to do work below their ability. They feel the hardship of life more vividly and find it difficult to be social or mix with others.

Number eleven

Eleven is a two and made up of two ones. It is a more individualised, double creative – impulsive to do big inspirational things and express itself as a teacher – and it is an inspirer of humanity. The general aspect is refined, inquisitive and able to inspire surroundings and express idealism. This number looks for the development of the highest and the best.

The negative aspect of this number would be seen in individuals who are depressed. People who live with little spiritual development and have issues discovering their own ideals and optimism. They could be insane or suffer from religious obsession.

Number three

Positive: lucky, natural, versatile, sociable, optimistic, gift of words, creative, emotional, seeking perfection.

Negative: wasteful, outspoken, gossipy, extravagant, opinionated, vain, wasteful, patronising.

Symbol: Jupiter. Positive aspect: Zodiac sign of Sagittarius, 21st November – 20th December. Negative aspect: Zodiac sign of Pisces, 19th February – 20th March.

This number is introvert.

Weekday: Thursday.

The number of ambition, style, people who want to go ahead in the world. The number for personal expression. They are willing to work hard and have a strong sense of duty. Lucky number and attract money easily. They bring joy, are enthusiastic, enjoy entertainment, society and make dreams come true. They are observant. They have a keen mind, are critical, learn quickly and easily. They are at their best when they can be creative and use their imagination. They are optimistic and are good communicators. They have the gift of the speech and the use of words, which can take them far. This vibration is always necessary to the success of the vibrations of 1 and 2.

The negative aspect of this number would be seen by individuals who repress their artistic ability or don't take advantage of opportunities that come their way. They often scatter their energy and don't stick with anything for very long. They simply cannot make up their mind how they would like to express themselves.

Number four

Positive: practical, stable, efficient, foundation, construction, serious, form, order, discipline.

Negative: dull, gloomy, careless, suspicious, exacting, argumentative, rigid, stubborn, slow.

Symbol: Uranus, the Sun. Positive aspect: Zodiac sign of Leo, 21st July – 20th August.

This number is extrovert.

Weekday: Sunday.

Four is the number for foundation, the builders of society – the number for materiality, the home. They give life form, but they must learn systems, and want facts and organisation. They have to work hard, are solid, positive, practical, have endurance and are respectable. Close attention to technicalities, physical and mental work. They are trustworthy, reliable and calm. They are thoughtful, considerate and loyal to their family. They cannot be selfish and must give service. They have a scientific mind and will obey law and order. A successful wage earner.

The negative aspect of this number would be seen by individuals who just live and work from day to day. They don't look for personal advancement in any way.

Number twenty-two

This number is more adaptable to practical, physical and intellectual expression than the other master number 11. Its ability is unlimited in understanding, and in its expression or illustration of an idea. They will be understood by people of all walks of life and can demonstrate practically the fundamental principles of truth. They are successful inventors of mechanical improvements.

The negative aspect of this number would be seen by individuals who just do insignificant work in the commercial world and are often disorganised and uncooperative. People who excessively inflate their ideas or their positions in life.

Number five

Positive: adventurous, resilient, sexual, resourceful, freedom, progress, versatility, new direction.

Negative: restlessness, nervous, temper, dissatisfaction, impulsiveness, impatience, instability, bizarre.

Symbol: Mercury. Positive aspect: Zodiac sign of Gemini 21st May – 20th June. Negative aspect: Zodiac sign of Virgo 21st August – 20th September.

page 172

This number is introvert.

Weekday: Wednesday.

They are adventurers and like anything exciting and new. They want life experience and personal liberty. They have many talents, and are versatile, resilient. They like a gamble and take chances. Full of life. Unafraid of experiences, they are attracted by everything and like to enjoy freedom in many forms. They must learn to be responsible and constructive, and not scatter their forces too much. They are very interested in what happens in the world, like to travel and be active. Great in the public as promoters, natural salesman and all lines of entertainment. They are adaptable and love variety and change, as long as it is forward moving. They do well to act upon inspiration.

The negative aspect of this number would be seen by individuals dominated by self-indulgence who lack the strength to overcome this habit.

Number six

Positive: domestic, harmony, honest, loyal, responsible, humanitarian, artist, idealist, marriage.

Negative: complacent, gossip, self-sacrifice, duty, outspokenness, nervous, upset, weakness, loser.

Symbol: Venus. Positive aspect: Zodiac sign of Taurus 20th April – 20th May. Negative aspect: Zodiac sign of Libra 21st September – 20th October.

This number is extrovert.

Weekday: Friday.

This number stands for cosmic adjustment, family, love and harmony. They are loyal, enjoy substantial friends and are very reliable. They are the natural helpers. They are fair, conscientious and take responsibility. They are intelligent and open-minded. They are teachers and healers, and love truth and justice. All methods of service, healing, friendship and love are expressed in the family and community. They have the possibility of artistic achievement. Art, beauty and cultural interests play a big part in their makeup. They finish whatever they undertake and are thorough in execution. High regard for morality and honesty.

The negative aspect of this number would be seen by individuals who become dependent on a stronger person. People who are homesick away from their country, family and home. People who show anxiety or feel overburdened by the responsibilities of care for relations or other human beings, often imposed upon them by others.

Number seven

Positive: mystical, intellectual, secretive, solitary, thinker, understanding, analysis, science, occult.

Negative: aloof, moody, confused, depressive, temper, cynic, suspicion, shrewdness, perfectionist.

Symbol: Neptune. Positive aspect: Zodiac sign of Cancer 21st June – 20th July.

This number is introvert.

Weekday: Monday.

They need to spend time alone, and rest. Solitary people, awkward among strangers but must learn not to feel isolated. Analytical and thinkers. They possess a lot of knowledge, understanding, spiritual awareness. They look for the hidden in everything and the reason why. They are intuitive, imaginative and have depth of feeling. They find it difficult to express their thoughts and ideas. They are inclined not to talk about themselves or their own private affairs. They are quiet and reserved, but draw unexpected help and assistance in surprising ways to them. They have a love for nature.

The negative aspect of this number would be seen by individuals who have a fear of failure and believe that no one understands them or even wants them. They feel disadvantaged and believe they never had a chance. They can't express their own inner thoughts. They have an inner concern for loneliness.

Number eight

Positive: tough, materialistic, tenacious, powerful, strong, capable, judgmental, supervision, efficiency.

Negative: ruthless, obstinate, ambitious, tense, clumsy, materialistic, uncaring, impatient, hard.

Symbol: Saturn. Positive aspect: Zodiac sign of Capricorn 21st December – 20th January. Negative aspect: Zodiac sign of Aquarius 21st January – 21st February .

This number is extrovert.

Weekday: Saturday.

They are good in the business world and like to enjoy material freedom. The material things in life are emphasised and they are able to solve all material problems. They have sound judgment in business. They need to find some balance with the material and spiritual needs of life, but they find this often hard to achieve to their satisfaction. The rewards of life are not easily obtained. They need a purpose or a goal that services the community or world. They possess strong characters and are wise and tenacious. They work hard, and have excellent mental powers and good judgment. They achieve positions of authority and power, which brings them happiness.

The negative aspect of this number would be seen by individuals who go bankrupt, lack material freedom and are unsuccessful in investment or speculation. People who have problems finding the higher positions in the business world.

Number nine

Positive: humanitarian, impulsive, unorthodox, forgiving, brotherhood, selfless, perfectionist, warm.

Negative: fickle, intolerant, deceptive, moody, personal interests, possessive, quarrelsome, bitter.

Symbol: Mars. Positive aspect: Zodiac sign of Aries 21st March – 19th April. Negative aspect: Zodiac sign of Scorpio 21st October – 20th November .

This number is introvert.

Weekday: Tuesday.

The highest number brings courage, a selfless attitude and care for brotherhood. This number stands for completion. They receive great satisfaction from giving to mankind. They must give without the need for reward. Their manner of expression is guided by the heart rather than the mind. They must learn the sheer pleasure of giving, being truly selfless and humanitarian. They don't care for possessions. They must grow in compassion, tolerance and forgiveness, and understand loss, sorrow and disappointment. They are divinely protected and have unlimited opportunities. They have the power within to succeed again and again. They need to be true to their ideals at all times. They express themselves artistically, emotionally and passionately. They demand freedom in action and thought for themselves and others.

The negative aspect of this number would be seen by individuals who take on the troubles of others, are over-emotional or over-generous, or impose themselves on others and are unable to look after themselves.

The way of life

Nothing great
was ever achieved
without enthusiasm.
The way of life
is wonderful;
it is by abandonment.

There is no limit
to what can be
accomplished
if it doesn't matter
who gets the credit.

Ralph Waldo Emerson

Notes

page 178

Chapter 20

Personal years 1-9, 11/2, 22/4 and Universal

page 180

First calculate your own Personal Year for the Universal Year you are living, and from that you can read about your right action for the year in this chapter, for the months in Chapter 21 and for the days in Chapter 22. Always reduce all sums to a single digit except the numbers 11 and 22.

Add the number of the **day** you are born, to the number of the **month** you are born, to the number of this **Universal Year** you are living. This will give you your **Personal Year** for the Universal Year you are living.

Example:

Born 25 December	(25)	2 + 5 = 7
December	(12)	1 + 2 = 3
Universal Year	(2013)	2 + 1 + 3 = 6
Total		7 + 3 + 6 = 16
Single digit	(16)	1 + 6 = 7

Personal year number seven during 2013 for Universal Year number six during 2013.

The **Universal Year** is calculated by adding the numbers of the **living year** down a single digit, except for numbers 11 and 22.

For example: 2009 is 2 + 9 = 11/2 Universal year

2013 is 2 + 1 + 3 = 6 Universal year

We can never forget the Universal Vibration, which is always around us and has a significant impact on our lives. We must always understand and integrate both our Personal and Universal Vibration. As an example in Christchurch the Universal energy caused the natural disaster, which has a great impact on your daily, monthly and yearly life. We make our own lives, decide our own choices, and if we live on the positive side of our own personal vibration we can live our own very Best Life and have everything we possibly want.

Eckhart Tolle, author of *The Power of Now* shows that the Universal vibration is very much interconnected and all around us.:

> The ultimate purpose of the world lies not within the world
> but in transcendence of the world. It is through the world and
> ultimately through you that the Unmanifested knows itself.
> You are here to enable the divine purpose of the Universe to unfold.

Universal Year 1: The world would be interested in new ventures. We would look for planning the future. We are very creative, with exploration and invention coming to the front. We want progress.

Personal Year 1: A year to start something new, have your own ideas, look for new beginnings, make changes, energise and expand – an action year.

Personal Year One

This year is your time to start a new cycle, with new beginnings and levels. It demands your action – go with the flow, take yourself out of your comfort zone and try new experiences. You need to have courage and make some plans for your future. You need to make the changes for progress and happiness. You are at a crossroad and there will be opportunities you have been waiting for. You feel very powerful and are determined. You must plant your seeds in the ground, which represent your goals. You will reap later what you sow and you must start now; don't be lazy. You need something new to go forward this year.

You need to become organised if you are to get the results in the future. You need a purpose or a new level, and it needs your clear thinking and strength. It is your year, you are in charge. Try to broaden your activities, meet all unexpected circumstances. You must show what you have and what you can do.

Take a chance on a new project; study the plans, your wisdom is needed. When called upon to make decisions use your intuitive, it must feel great to you. Keep moving forward throughout the year.

Hard work may be necessary to get a project up and running. Get it done so you can be the individual you have the potential to be. Your power is high this year. Be confident and assertive; important changes are likely, but it needs your effort. It's your time to break free, be yourself and keep life moving forward.

Universal Year 2: A year to work on cooperation and to use diplomacy in all political negotiations. We collect and draw up agreements. We must build peace and harmony between nations. We work in association with others and develop balance in all our dealings with each other.

Universal Year 11/2: A year for spiritual teachings. Much interest is shown in spiritualism and all forms of occultism. The world needs a vision for the betterment of mankind.

Personal Year 2: A year to plan and research, to develop partnership, to be patient, to cooperate, to be diplomatic, to pay attention to all the small, new beginnings, and to be tactful. A slow year.

Personal Year 11/2: A year when the emotions are stronger. You feel more tested on your sensitivity. Your main concern is inner growth and to create a vision for yourself. See Personal Year Two.

Personal Year Two

This year is a much slower year for you. You need to show patience in all your interactions with others. You will experience more obstacles and limitations in your dealings with them. You need to become cooperative, diplomatic and adaptable. This is especially necessary when things don't run smoothly. You will be observant and quick in receiving ideas.

Everything is still very much in its early stages of development. It needs planning, research and attention to detail. You will need to wait for any results of projects and developments. Everything needs time and can't be pushed forward or challenged too much. Any attempt to force issues will most likely bring disharmony, delay and broken partnerships. Instead find a way to keep calm, pleasant and cooperative and this could bring results beyond your expectation.

New partnerships, friends or even a love relationship can be realised this way. It will be important to decide what help and support you need for your plans. You may find different routes to work on your new projects, so stay open-minded – this way you will gain valuable insight into your purpose and direction. Give yourself the time to study all plans and obtain new information on subjects that interest you. You may feel much limitation and be more sensitive this year.

Trust things will come to you. If you feel the need, look for people who can help you with clarity in your career or personal relationships. This way you will gain much confidence and be better equipped for the future.

Personal Year 11/2

The same as Personal Year Two, but you could feel more tested on your sensitivity. This is not a weakness but rather a strength – to understand people and to have the possibility to look into the souls of others. You feel very intuitive, and you should trust this. Much nervous tension could be experienced, so find a way to balance yourself through deep breathing and meditation. You also might be more inclined to concentrate on experiences involving religious, spiritual, psychic and occult matters. Your concern is with inside growth.

Universal Year 3: A year to create a sense of joy. We look more at the lighter side of life, putting emphasis on social life and entertainment. Expansion for theatres and all places of amusement. We spend money and feel restless. We scatter our forces, maybe to the point of recklessness.

Personal Year 3: A year to have fun, to be social and develop your friendships, to make new friends, to be creative about what you're planning to do, to stay centred and look for self-improvement. A go-with-the-flow year.

Personal Year Three

page 185

This year you must become more creative and imaginative with your plans. All this will improve your finances and make for happier relationships. Your friends old and new will be important and of value. This is a good time for entertainment and social activities. Be open and accept invitations. Communication will play a big part in your success this year. Any writing in a constructive way is beneficial. Be joyful, optimistic and fun this year. You will experience more personal freedom to do all those things you want to accomplish.

Watch out for taking on too many projects at a time; finish one before starting another. Try not to scatter your energies and stay in charge of your own time. It is a good time to pay attention to self-improvement and to go on a journey of self-discovery. Find some new personal and business networks.

Mostly be happy and work on not being too emotionally involved in all your relationships. Instead enjoy them, be helpful, be a good friend but don't forget what is personally important to you. It is your time to believe in yourself and focus on your own dreams.

Universal Year 4: A year to face financial difficulties and economic problems. Shortage of employment. We need to work on and build a secure, strong foundation for lasting success.

Universal Year 22/4: Practical achievements for the good of the world. Big ideas, big growth.

Personal Year 4: A year to work hard, to focus, to take action, to dig deep, to be practical. Take care of details that will bring a sense of purpose and destiny and give form to your idea. A slow year.

Personal Year 22/4: A year to put all your dreams into practical use for the benefit of humanity at large. We must not put attention on personal advancement. A good chance to do something big for the good of the world.

Personal Year Four

A year to become serious about your wishes. Opportunities will be there to meet and make happen. This is a time to be practical and reliable, to stop dreaming and being indulgent with yourself. Overall developments will be slow, but it is your time to place strong foundations, so that a stable and secure future can be built upon your life.

It's a great time to think of order, system and good management to establish firmer conditions in your life. You look for security in most areas of your life, such as relationships, career, living conditions, health and business. It will need your energy, common sense, time, discipline and strong character to keep seriously working at each task to help you to go forward.

This is a good time to buy, sell, build and exchange. It will be important to make sure it meets your standards and values. The year asks you to focus on your commitments and responsibilities.

It is important to be aware of your assets, mortgages, leases and to think up a budget – even try to pay up. Any contract that ask for signing, make sure you investigate it – be vigilant around it and always read the fine print. You can't take anything on face value, so check and check again.

Personal Year 22/4

The same as Personal Year four. This year you must put your dreams into practical use. The universe at large is felt and not much concern for personal gain is to be had. However there are great possibilities and progress for significant projects and ventures. Status and recognition may result. Financial gain may accrue if motives are for brotherhood and mankind. Put on your full effort and don't procrastinate. A good time to do something big for the good in this world. Humanity is the focus all year.

Universal Year 5: We find better working conditions. International activities in commerce and trade. Dynamic progress, interest in new and unusual ventures. In general a sense of excitement and adventure, an urge towards rejuvenation.

Personal Year 5: A year to make changes for progress, to think new people and a new job, to adapt, to take a risk, to promote and advertise, maybe even to take a leap. An active year.

Personal Year Five

page 188

This year you will want to feel free. After all the hard work of the last year you must make room for new things to come into your life. You need to know what is happening in the world. A great time to travel, visit places and meet people. Go out of your comfort zone and break away from routine. A good time for adventure and fun activities. Though try not to overindulge too much in the best things in life such as food, alcohol and sensual pleasures.

If you have a business, promote it – look for different ways to brand it. Any advertising is money well spent. It's a time for progress and growth. You can start new projects or put attention to new interests.

Take advantage of new opportunities and new conditions, be adaptable, go forward and don't stand still. Even take a risk or leap – your foundations were laid last year. Any transformation will be calculated.

You may change and improve your environment, buy or sell properties, have new relationships, new ideas, new plans. Somehow it will be related to the old, but it will create more success and a broader field of interest and activity. An important change is likely this year.

Try to avoid being restless, scattering you energy in all directions or being impatient. Also don't run away from old commitments – work through them and don't burn your bridges behind you. Good judgment is always necessary; confusion could lead to legal problems.

Changes can be unexpected; go with the flow, be adaptable and you will benefit greatly.

You cannot completely control the outcome from your choices. Without movement in our lives we miss out on important opportunities for growth and progress.

Universal Year 6: We consider international responsibilities and duties. We look to advance education and health conditions. Emphasis on harmonising family life and regulating home economics.

Personal Year 6: A year to take care of responsibilities and duties, often around the home and family. Look for deeper meaning, truth and love, to give service and to work for beauty and harmony. A slower year.

Personal Year Six

You are now past halfway in your nine-year cycle. This year you will feel the responsibilities and duties more, and often they are coming from the family or your community. You start to see the results of all your planning and efforts for your important goals.

You look for love or wish to deepen your close relationships. It's an excellent year for marriage, love and romance. There will be divorce if love is betrayed or is not lived up to. Legal problems can occur if justice and truth is not practised.

Your home is important and any maintenance requirements you must attend to. You work on harmony and balance in all your relationships. Be very thorough and conscientious about everything you do and finish all undertakings. Avoid procrastination.

Service is the key to getting the best result in everything you do this year. Goodwill towards others is asked for – to think and work only for the self will bring disappointments and regret. The possibility for better financial returns is there. Any expense and bills relating to duty and responsibility must and can be fulfilled at all times. Take care of your own health as well as that of others. It is, after all, your duty year.

Put your attention to justice, fair play and honesty. Your feelings of what is right and wrong are strong; always try to avoid misunderstandings, difficulties and arguments. You could become involved in teaching, coaching, counselling or being the peacemaker at work as well as in domestic relationships.

Universal Year 7: A year for quiet thinking, inward searching and studies, but no new ventures. Rather give a finished quality to everything we've undertaken. Spiritual, religious and occult interest and expansion.

Personal Year 7: A year to spend some time with you – to obtain great inner personal growth, to analyse, to read, study past and present, to meditate. No casual associations; instead go for deeper meaning, to reflect and plan for the future. A very low-energy year.

page 190

Personal Year Seven

This year you must reflect on and analyse your life. It's a good time to spend time alone, to study, research and meditate. Maybe you will teach and write about technical, scientific, religious and occult subjects. Develop your inner power and spiritual awareness. Your inner growth comes to the front and changes your way of thinking and feeling. You look for perfection, beauty and a higher level of thought and action. You want to be free from all the duties and responsibilities of last year. Control any feelings of limitation or confusion.

It is your time; you become the focus. Even the big crowds feel more overwhelming than ever before. You start to enjoy spending time with yourself or with just a few others. Unexpected rewards can come to you now, which will give you a great feeling for being at the right place at the right time. Go with the flow. The teacher arrives when the student is ready. Not a year to force any issues; instead be ready when it arrives at your doorstep.

Gain strength through rest and quiet times. Your energy feels lower. You will gain confidence in yourself; trust in your intuition and in your ability to do good in this world. Learn about life and its deeper meaning. Read inspirational and self-help books, enjoy nature, exercise yoga and meditate. Be poised, say little – just let life happen at the moment. Life will unfold naturally and surprise you in very unexpected ways. Any health matters need attention and looking into.

In business grow better – go deeper, not bigger. Get away from business pressures. It's not a good time for change, just reflection and perfection. Study the past and the present, and plan for the future. Finance will come when it is needed, always just in time. Await developments; take little action and don't force anything.

Universal Year 8: We enjoy prosperity and expansion. No shortage of jobs and money. Increased business activity and a sense of material wellbeing. Development of commercial relations with foreign countries. Huge amalgamations are possible.

Personal Year 8: A year to accomplish, to work hard, to go after new projects, to be fair and honest, to take action, and to advance and improve your standing. A business and finance year. A very active year.

Personal Year Eight

This year is your power year. Your time for material accomplishments and financial success. A time for rewards and recognition. Now you must take action to achieve your goals. You must make it happen. You feel empowered, strong and in charge. You are ready to move forward in a businesslike manner with resourcefulness, authority, executive ability, good judgement and efficiency. It is your time for accomplishments and to take advantage of any situation that arises.

Opportunities are there for you, so seek them out. You feel self-confident, have the skills, and are in charge, and it will all lead to your success and financial gain. Get advice from those in authority if needed. Financial matters need to be taken into account and organised. It's important not to overestimate your ability or to be careless with money; instead be realistic and grounded. Hard work will lead to results and you will be rewarded.

In this busy year when there are many demands upon your time and judgment take time out to rest and attend to health matters.

Take control of your personal and professional life. It is an excellent time for business and financial activities. Get the promotion you always wanted. Put your house on the market and it will sell. You can make things happen now. Feel the power of accomplishment. It's your time, so put your leadership skills to good use and make your goals a reality.

Universal Year 9: We need to finish what we have started. Love and brotherhood is cultivated. Selfishness and greed cannot flourish. The old must be finalised all the while the universe keeps moving and growing.

Personal Year 9: A year to finish, to de-clutter, to stay focused and to contemplate future plans. Take action only in order to complete something. Celebrate your achievements over the last nine years. A year with both low and high energy.

Personal Year Nine

The last year of this cycle, it is a time to finish everything you have started during this period and to start contemplating a new beginning next year. First you need to finish with the old and that way you make room for the new to come in. Anything that has no further value to you any more, let it go or finish it.

You need to pay up your bills, make the calls you have to make. It is not always an easy year; emotions may run high. You must complete, forgive and be tolerant in all matters. Friendships will be evaluated, business or personal. Some you will deepen; with others you will look for completion or ask for freedom. Try not to challenge these; let them go – you don't need them for the future. Overall the year will be full of love and happiness.

Finish or let go of all inspirational endeavours you have started, such as that book you are writing. It's definitely also a great time to look for any creative actions like music and the arts.

All year be helpful to others and you will be rewarded. At times give life a chance to help you. Avoid being selfish and personal; instead keep your mind open for broader interests. You must be prepared for much drama and emotion.

This is not a good time to start new issues, especially something major like a new business. Activities started in this year often end prematurely. Don't overwork yourself and look after your health.

At all times, if something goes out of your life let it go – it is the way to your future happiness. An important change is likely this year, by your own or others' effort.

No action, no result

You may never know
What results come
from your actions,
But if you do nothing,
There will be no result.

Mahatma Gandhi

Notes

page 194

Chapter 21

Personal month in Personal year 1-9, 11/2, 22/4 and Universal

page 196

First calculate your own Personal Year for the Universal Year you are living in (Refer to Chapter 20). Reduce the calendar month October (10th month) to 1, November (11th month) to 2 and December (12th month) to 3. This month has more force than the single-numbered months January, February and March.

Your **Personal Month** is calculated by adding the **Calendar Month** to your **Personal Year**.

For example, if your Personal Year is 7, the Calendar Month is December (12th month adds up to 3),

$$7 \text{ (PY)} + 3 \text{ (CM)} = 7 + 3 = 10 \text{ continue to reduce } 1 + 0 = 1$$

Therefore the month December in your Personal Year seven has a vibration of number one for you.

Find on pages 200 to 241 the details for every Personal Month in all Personal Years, substitute the months in Personal Year 11/2 and 22/4 respectively for Personal Year 2 and 4. Some details for 11/2 are found in February and for 22/4 in April.

The **Universal Month** is found by adding the **Calendar Month** to the **Universal Year**.

For example, Calendar Month December (12th month adds up to 3), in the Universal Year 2013 (2 + 1 + 3 = 6),

$$3 \text{ (CM)} + 6 \text{ (UY)} = 3 + 6 = 9$$

This means that December in 2013 has a Universal vibration of number nine for everyone.

Find on pages 200 to 241 the detail for every Universal Month in the nine-year cycle.

Always reduce all sums to a single digit except the numbers 11 and 22.

As you live your life and follow your own personal direction for the month, also take the Universal vibration of the Calendar Month into account. This will have an influence on you as well.

We can never forget the Universal vibration, which is always around us and has a significant impact on our lives. We must always understand and integrate both our Personal and Universal vibration. As an example in Christchurch the Universal energy caused the natural disaster, which has a great impact on your daily, monthly and yearly life. However we make our own lives, decide our own choices, and if we live on the positive side of our own personal vibration we can live our own very Best Life and have everything we could possibly want.

The chart of the nine-year cycle, month by month, is as follows.

Years 1 to 9

Months	**1**	**2**	**3**	**4**	**5**	**6**	**7**	**8**	**9**
1 January	2	3	4	5	6	7	8	9	1
2 February	3	4	5	6	7	8	9	1	2
3 March	4	5	6	7	8	9	1	2	3
4 April	5	6	7	8	9	1	2	3	4
5 May	6	7	8	9	1	2	3	4	5
6 June	7	8	9	1	2	3	4	5	6
7 July	8	9	1	2	3	4	5	6	7
8 August	9	1	2	3	4	5	6	7	8
9 September	1	2	3	4	5	6	7	8	9
(10)1 October	2	3	4	5	6	7	8	9	1
(11)2 November	3	4	5	6	7	8	9	1	2
(12)3 December	4	5	6	7	8	9	1	2	3

It is interesting to note that the last two months of each year are the same number as the first two months in the following year. You could conclude nothing ends or begins all at once.

The month September carries the number of the Personal Year you are living, which brings the full force of the Personal Year to work in all your endeavours. Also, as you can see, October will always carry the number for your next Personal Year. This could mean a little advance notice for the year to come. Maybe you could plan ahead, but the plans cannot get fully under way until the next year starts. First you must complete your current year, the one you are living in.

During the first five years, a full cycle of nine is never fully worked out without interruption.

During the sixth year, one complete cycle is finished, another not fully developed.

During the seventh year only one cycle is fully developed, with two other cycles being partially completed,.

During the eighth year, notice the sudden ending of a partial cycle in January.

During the ninth year, two cycles are begun, only one completed.

Taking note of all this will help you greatly with being in charge of your own life. It helps with planning for future happenings. You start to understand life and possibly work with it better, so you don't feel as challenged or stressed at different times in your life. Everything is a passing stage. You have a way to plan what to do, when and how, month by month and year after year. You also start to understand the people close to you better. Life is a puzzle, but you are always in charge – you make the choices – and this will help you to do it well in your OWN Best Life. Have fun, work with it, and decide for yourself if it has meaning for you. It is science, so it will always need research. The Universe is mysterious; let's try to find a way to explain the unexplainable.

Any feedback is very welcome, so thank you in advance.

Month: January

Universal Month Number One

In this month we introduce and get started on our new plans and ideas. Pioneers and inventors are discovered. Leaders are appointed. New committees are formed.

Personal Year Number One

You will want to plan for improvement in your way of living and in regard to your home and business affairs. Start with making an effort to move forward mentally. Be willing to cooperate as to ways and means. Relationships may need some attention. Study and look into all the details of your plans. There is no need to rush. Take time out for social activities.

Personal Year Number Two

Friends and social activities are important this month. Follow your own interests and be creative but keep new ideas and plans to yourself for now. Work on your self-confidence. Surround yourself with optimistic and success-minded individuals. There could be unexpected pleasures or surprises in the association and in the help they can give you. Romance is in the air.

Personal Year Number Three

A practical month – there are many things to do and to attend to. Give problems attention in order to gain better management and order. Establish a detailed action plan for important projects and goals. It is wise not to argue or to act emotionally; rather act upon any issues in a sensible manner. Always look for harmony and avoid unhappy reactions. Start a healthy daily routine.

Personal Year Number Four

It will take time to work out all the things you want to do. You may receive practical offers and face opportunities, but make sure they count towards the future not just for the moment only. Avoid hasty decisions. There is the possibility of a trip or social activities. Take some time out to prepare for the hard work in the coming months. Enjoy friends and live up to family responsibilities.

Personal Year Number Five

Changes are in the air. You will value your freedom more than usual. This is a good time to develop new personal and business relationships. It's a time to accept responsibilities and to talk things over. Any problems or conditions need to be carefully thought through. This is not the time for arguing. The duty is yours and must be accepted at this time. Take care of your health.

Personal Year Number Six

You need some alone time this month. It is wise to do a lot of thinking – to relax, read, meditate and have long walks in the woods. Balance and harmony in all aspects of your life are most important. Think about how you want your home and family life to improve this year. Look after health matters – your own or those of someone else in the family.

Personal Year Number Seven

A busy month to finish off loose ends to do with property, business or other possessions. You are still dealing with some duty and responsibility from last year. It's important to do what is necessary to get results, and much expense will be connected with this. However enough money will be at hand to work out your plans. You experience more self-assurance, and a new opportunity may also be present.

Personal Year Number Eight

You will make a rather strong decision about your property or possessions. You are in a better position to make choices that are in tune with your inner purpose. Legal affairs may enter into. Don't force issues; instead use compassion, tolerance and forgiveness. An opportunity will present itself to help you to get ready for the potential of great accomplishment. Avoid feelings of uncertainty.

Personal Year Number Nine

There are many loose ends to take care of before you can feel the freedom the year will bring to you. Keep all doubts and fears under control. Review your life during the past eight years and choose in your heart what you would like to keep. Acknowledge what you have learned, and slowly new plans will begin to take form in your mind and heart. Show tolerance and compassion.

Month: February

Universal Month Number Two

In this month we collect materials and compile statistics. We use diplomacy and tact in politics.

Universal Month Number 11/2

In this month there will be activity in cults, churches, temples, synagogues and missions. Spiritual values will be expressed.

Personal Year Number One

This month move forward for general improvement, and add inspiration and imagination to your work. You are much more optimistic and are open for new opportunities. This is a time to be friendly and sociable, to meet up with friends. Through this help will become available to you. Avoid impulsive and headstrong actions. Buy something new, take a short vacation, give a party – and most of all enjoy yourself.

Personal Year Number Two

A month to work hard, with the need to focus on details. It's a good time to go ahead with your personal plans. Take care of money and financial matters. At all times show courtesy, diplomacy and cooperation. This way you work in harmony with others and you establish a solid basis for further progress and your own good. Take care of your health and that of family and friends.

Personal Year Number 11/2

A year for spiritual vision and inner growth. You will feel more sensitive. Balance your energy through meditation and deep breathing, and find inner calm. Religion, higher thought, and psychic and spiritual experiences are possible. A time for inner growth. Show an interest in the general welfare and betterment of society.

Personal Year Number Three

This is a good time to make changes for progress, growth and expansion. Keep in mind your own personal wishes. For best results be practical and guard yourself against being overconfident or restless. At all times keep control of your emotions and be mindful of careless words and conversation. A great time to take action; do not wait for others to help you right now.

Personal Year Number Four

A very busy month, with the focus on organising your home, family and business affairs. It's best to be helpful, but do not take on more than is right or fair. Family matters must be taken care of. Good experiences will come through your willingness to do the work and meet your responsibilities. Relationships are stable now. Look after your health and keep your finances in check.

Personal Year Number Five

Find time to be alone – to meditate and be quiet. Deepen your understanding of your life purpose and direction. Think things out to a logical conclusion; avoid being emotional. Nothing is to be gained from being demanding, forcing issues or doing too much talking. Better results will come if you remain sensitive and diplomatic. Always work on a solid plan for the future. Take care of your health and diet.

Personal Year Number Six

Business and money management call for organisation and efficiency. Significant results may be achieved now. Much needs to be considered regarding houses and property. Expenses will have to be managed, but help will come through friends or associates. Watch your money; put some aside and keep to a budget. There is the possibility of a business trip and the meeting of old friends.

Personal Year Number Seven

Some of your tasks, relationships and duties must change; others will finish through your own actions or through outside conditions. This is a good time to think clearly and to look at what you want for yourself. Your actions will influence your thoughts, so don't allow yourself to be confused or out of sorts. The best way is warmth of feeling, tolerance and compassion, and to get ready for a new setup.

Personal Year Number Eight

Time to take action – to step up and go ahead with your plans, whether they be family or business. Very soon things will fall into place, so stay focused on your talents and abilities, and be more creative in the way you express yourself. Take problems in your stride and take the initiative. This is a time to go ahead with a good plan. You can make money or receive the help you need to go forward.

Personal Year Number Nine

A month to be social and to make new friends. You feel vulnerable and sensitive in personal relationships. For the best results use patience, diplomacy and a willingness to share. Always keep poised and happy. If necessary obtain good advice from outside your own circles. Don't try to work things out entirely by your own ideas, and don't take yourself too seriously – relax some.

Notes

page 206

Month: March

Universal Month Number Three

In this month we find activity in the market. There will be amusements, fun and friends, and you'll be busy on committees.

Personal Year Number One

Work hard on your new projects and goals. You need to get focused and organised, and take care of the necessary details. Be responsible – this is no time for dreaming. Overcome emotions and resentment. Avoid arguments and disagreements. Family projects call for your attention. Take care of your own health and diet, and find some time to rest.

Personal Year Number Two

A time to go forward. However be cooperative and take care of legal matters. Avoid risky ventures and stay away from get-rich-quick schemes. This is a great time for new interests and people. Take a trip and buy something new. Be prepared for the unexpected and use diplomacy rather than force to win over the opposition. It's not wise to talk out of turn or argue.

Personal Year Number Three

You have to consider others with your plans, and maintain balance in all activities. Talk things over for a better understanding and for the good of all concerned. Your creative approach to problem-solving is appreciated by others. You must meet your obligations and duties and get down to work. Take time to do all the necessary little things. Pleasant connections will make this month interesting.

Personal Year Number Four

This month say very little and find time to get away. Rest, relax, read, write or study, and through meditation and deep thought you will work things out well. Reflect on your goals – are you on track? Under all circumstances avoid arguing about anything and always eliminate misunderstandings. Instead go ahead with skill – you are able to solve complex problems with sensitivity.

Personal Year Number Five

This is a good time for a change and to plan for action to bring more personal freedom and opportunity – definitely not a time to let matters drift. It is important to obtain advice when investing money or assets. Make contact with people in authority or who have influence. Finances will improve a little. Use wisdom and patience – it's important to meet the opposition with genuine consideration for the best result.

Personal Year Number Six

Make new friends and enjoy the old ones. Keep an eye open for new opportunities and helpful new ideas. You may be drawn to participate in a community or volunteer project. Take some rest and look after your health. This is a very good time to complete your unfinished projects. Most of all though, be charming and show tolerance and understanding to your fellow human beings.

Personal Year Number Seven

This is a good time to go ahead with new plans and to look to the future. An excellent time to begin studies, reading, meditation, yoga etc. Enjoy being busy and doing different things. Most of all have a deep inner poise and keep faith for good results. Avoid getting involved in the domestic and business problems of others; instead stay kind and look for harmony.

Personal Year Number Eight

Be social, enjoy networking and be warm and friendly towards your friends, colleagues and associates. Moving forward is dependent on others, so keep your emotions to yourself and balance yourself. Some delays this month, but at all times keep your goal in mind. Always show patience and understanding. You will need help and intelligent advice for best results and more personal freedom.

Personal Year Number Nine

You will have more freedom this month to find the opportunity to do some of the things you want to do. You are feeling more optimistic about the future. Enjoy a vacation, some social activities, parties and old friends. You may take up a new short-term line of work or study. Cultivate your interest in art and creative enterprises. Always show tolerance and compassion for the best result in everything you do.

Month: April

Universal Month Number Four

In this month skilled workers will find work. The focus is on steady careful building and training, and any mistakes will be corrected. Specialisation is needed and worked for.

Universal Month Number 22/4

In this month we experience boundless energy, internationally focused. There will be improved conditions for national work projects, railroads, waterways and international relationships.

Personal Year Number One

It's a good time to move forward with your personal plans. You will experience some freedom, which is giving you more opportunity to do what you want to do. A great opportunity may present itself. A good time for adventure and excitement. Travel is possible ,and prepare yourself for some surprises. Changes in living conditions or occupation may be made if you so wish to do.

Personal Year Number Two

Much duty and responsibility towards family, home and loved ones is required. Be kind and helpful to those who depend on you and maybe arrange a romantic getaway. Use diplomacy and sensitivity in difficult situations. This will bring great reward and more harmonious relationships. Let go of conditions that are no longer necessary. You will gain more peace of mind this way.

Personal Year Number Three

Be very wise, avoid arguments and don't talk too much; keep poised. Find some time for meditation and inner reflection. This is a good time to think over and carefully plan your creative ideas. The best results will come through waiting and not forcing issues. Instead reflect on what you want in life and hold on to it. Unexpected gifts and nice things will be gained through having faith in the process.

Personal Year Number Four

A good month to buy, sell or trade, and to put your mind to getting things done. Your dedication, focus and hard work is paying off. This will give improvement in all matters of business, home and family affairs. Look at all details, keep a clear head and be prepared for surprises and the unexpected. Not a good time to trust to luck or chance. Best to remain practical and grounded, and stay confident.

Personal Year Number 22/4

A year to launch a huge project with significant influence in the world. You need to give service to all and consider international. You should take action. This way financial gain and recognition is possible. No personal gain. Mastery on the material plane. Nervous tension is likely.

Personal Year Number Five

Everything depends now on how you get on with others. A relationship may come to an end and some projects are coming to a close. Make it a win-win outcome for the best result. Be wise in all legal matters. Refuse to fight and argue. This is a good time to take a short trip or do something different. If the need is there for you to reorganise your plans and improve your health do it.

Personal Year Number Six

This month it's time to take action and move forward, to do all the things that are necessary to bring improvement. You feel positive and confident with your plans, but don't take on too much responsibility. Focus on your career and personal interest. Spend some time with family and friends. Bring some romance into your relationship or you could meet someone special.

Personal Year Number Seven

Great time for a study and to begin mental and spiritual discipline. Your intuition will be spot on and should be followed. This month don't talk too much about what you are working towards. Stay focused, and spend some time taking care of the details of your personal plans. Always show patience and cooperation with others. Take care of your health and nervous system.

Personal Year Number Eight

This month you will find time to do things for yourself. You feel optimistic and lucky. Your efforts and hard work are recognised. You should enjoy some pleasure, entertainment or a trip. Attend lectures, culture activities and spend some money. You will find inspiration and courage. However you always do need to apply good judgment, ability and efficiency to work, and use opportunities to get your results.

Personal Year Number Nine

Since this is a practical month, you may consider a move or a change of residence. A lot of things are coming to an end. All matters having to do with property, legal papers and agreements call for the best possible management and good judgment. Avoid being impatient and do not allow emotional unrest to rule you; instead use your good common sense. Take time out to rest and sleep, and always eat healthy foods.

Notes

page 214

Month: May

Universal Month Number Five

In this month we expect an increase in sales and advertising, plus speculation and expansion. New products will be on the market. There will be activity in the theatres.

Personal Year Number One

Work towards a balance in home and business; you do need to show responsibility and honour your duties. Any changes you want to make can be tried out. Always make sure you give your service happily and don't look at self-interest alone; act from the heart. The family, children and friends all seek your advice and sympathy. You can receive money, but also have many expenses.

Personal Year Number Two

It's advisable not to force any issues; stay poised and keep yourself control. Avoid resentment if results are not just what you expected or wanted. Make adjustments based on what you have learned. Be fair, and help will come in surprising ways. Take time to rest and relax and to think out everything, but always control your moods and feelings.

Personal Year Number Three

Business matters are ready for a new direction and improvement this month. Financial conditions need good judgment – don't be too emotional or overoptimistic. Be wise and keep yourself control to avoid going on the wrong track or spending more money than you should. Go forward with your realistic plans and take advantage of opportunities. Take care of your health.

Personal Year Number Four

A plan, undertaking, association or task may reach a natural conclusion. New ideas regarding the home, family and business are likely to influence your thinking. First finish the old arrangements before the new can get under way. Always keep cheerful, generous and helpful. Volunteer work will give reward. The whole year will demand work, routine, effort and patience.

Personal Year Number Five

New people and ideas may make for an interesting and exciting time. Be adventurous. Some unexpected conditions can work to your advantage. Your mind is more free and at ease now. Don't let other opinions concern you; be progressive in your own way. You can begin activities now, but avoid being hurried. However go forward – be enterprising, be bold and work towards the new direction.

Personal Year Number Six

Be cooperative in all your undertakings. This is a good time to discuss with others the details of plans and know what is what. By knowing the finer points, you may be able to turn things around and gain pleasing results. At all times be tactful and avoid all conflict, but be assertive. You are more sensitive and intuitive. Money conditions should be more settled. Enjoy some social activities.

Personal Year Number Seven

Follow the inspiration or impulse to do creative work, to study, write or read, or to give expression to your artistic feelings or your talents. Find an outlet for your ideas, which have been around in your mind and heart for a long time. Avoid moods or hurt feelings during emotional upsets caused by others. Instead use wisdom, be kind and helpful. Enjoy some fun and pleasure and be a good friend.

Personal Year Number Eight

Many things must be managed and put into place, so focus on the detail. It's necessary if you are to get results; all your efforts will pay off later in the year. Money will come. Be vigilant with signing papers or contracts. Ask advice from those who know. You will receive help this way. At all times stay focused and disciplined, and work hard on all projects and undertakings. Your family will call for care and consideration.

Personal Year Number Nine

You find yourself very busy and active in the middle of changes and inner transformation. You are excited and ready to experience new situations. You are looking forward to more personal freedom. While time is still a consideration, go ahead determinedly without making long-term commitments. Avoid arguments and disagreements, for they could upset you and disrupt your prepared plans.

Month: June

Universal Month Number Six

In this month we must give support to the community. Civic improvements. Health and wellbeing. Weddings. Education and balance in all activities.

Personal Year Number One

Take time out for self-analysis, reading, study and meditation. Make all your goals clear to yourself. Look for inspiration and a positive state of mind. Meet financial obligations and use good business judgement. Make sure all is fair and right for others and for yourself; otherwise make adjustments. Avoid arguments and criticism. Mostly try to relax, rest and take care of your health.

Personal Year Number Two

You feel stronger and more able to take care of business and life in general. You may consider changing your living conditions; just use good judgement, be efficient, keep control of emotions and consider cooperation. A trip for business or fun may be made. Financial conditions will be positive. At all times get good advice from those with influence and business experience.

Personal Year Number Three

You will realise that you are at the end of some work, task or personal relationship. It seems best to let go of things no longer needed. Property must be considered in a businesslike manner. You may wish to sell, but more time may be needed. However you will find this ending a release in some way and an emotional improvement in the end. Be compassionate and understanding.

Personal Year Number Four

You will be busy and determined with future plans about what you want and are going to do. Get the true facts to make the right decisions, and consider also your own ability. Move forward with practical plans, but always be businesslike and use good judgement. Economic conditions may be slow and demand attention; even a family crisis could need consideration or represent change.

Personal Year Number Five

There is a need to be patient, tactful and diplomatic to bring about fine results. Just be patient – there is more to be gained by helping and working with others. Results are not visible yet, but there is much going on underneath the surface. Other people are difficult to deal with and change seems to take time, but cooperation could produce the turning point and bring benefits in the future.

Personal Year Number Six

A good time to do things that interest you personally and give you inspiration. Take a trip or be at home, but indulge in creative and artistic work that have to do with the qualities of the soul and spirit. Spend a little money on yourself. Live up to your own ideas and ideals, but be careful of what you say and avoid gossip. The trend is for the advent of opportunities to go into business and make more money.

Personal Year Number Seven

There is work to be done so be practical – you may feel economic pressure, uninspired and let down, but you need to get things ready for the future. This is not a good time to take a vacation or to promote personal interests. Get your affairs in better order, say nothing, show patience, and do whatever has to be done to get the results you anticipate. Look after your health – you may feel a lack of energy.

Personal Year Number Eight

You will experience a feeling of freedom, accompanied by new interests or new people. You may travel for business or pleasure and look for new ideas in view of helping others. For best result don't speak impulsively; instead put your best foot forward. Always be alert and resourceful in meeting people or the public because there is something for you to gain through association or contact with many people.

Personal Year Number Nine

You may see some of the rewards or improvements that the closing cycle promises. More time is needed, and some affairs of the home and family will demand attention and time. You feel a lot of responsibility, but through being kind and helpful you will receive money and assistance. Too much self-determination and impatience will delay the real personal satisfaction you are looking for.

Notes

page 222

Month: July

Universal Month Number Seven

In this month we must examine, analyse and improve. Research and create. We will have better finances.

Personal Year Number One

page 224

A good time to be organised, disciplined and persuasive. Opportunity is there to take control of business and financial matters. Push forward, for this is a time to buy, sell or to arrange property matters, or alter business activities and living conditions. Meet up with friends and make new important business relationships. Always be diplomatic, have self-confidence and smile, and you will succeed.

Personal Year Number Two

Not the best time for personal self-seeking and commercial aggressiveness. Instead be forgiving and kind, and you will inspire, counsel and support others. The best results can only be accomplished through a tactful, diplomatic approach and to show patience. This is not the time to begin anything. Finish up loose ends and meet up with people who have the contacts or ability to further personal ambitions.

Personal Year Number Three

A time for new beginnings, situations and people, so this is a good time to take initiative and to make changes. Always make your decisions independently and intellectually. Life seems to be leading you in a new direction. However work towards inspirational and creative self-improvement. Always be friendly and make others happy and you will experience much harmony as well as some interesting contacts.

Personal Year Number Four

Most important this month are your interactions with friends and lovers. A great deal of tact and diplomacy is required. Take some rest and concentrate your attention on the little things you have overlooked lately. This month could bring a turning point. At all times be patient, gracious, adaptable and understanding as you wait developments. Always be willing to take responsibility to help others.

Personal Year Number Five

Time to be light-hearted and playful, and to go on a holiday. Look for an inspirational idea, make a creative effort, do something for self-improvement. All forms of communications are important, so be seen and heard. Call old friends and make new ones. For the most part be happy and have some fun. This is also a good time to show off your talents, but avoid impulsiveness and spending too much money.

Personal Year Number Six

Hard work will bring good results. Organise your time and energy, and follow through on commitments. Living conditions might change and you may do work or be interested in things you have never thought of before. Be efficient, meticulous and scrupulous in stabilising finances. Take care of your health, eating habits and physical fitness. This is a good time to produce tangible and pleasing results.

Personal Year Number Seven

The opportunity will be there to make transitions and changes. Take a trip, go places, do things, experience a sense of freedom. Now is the time to take a chance on love and luck. Find new people or in fact anything, that will bring variety and a renewed interest. Take time to do a lot of thinking and focus on self-analysis. Show interest in the mental and intellectual activities of the world.

Personal Year Number Eight

This is a month to focus on loved ones, your home and community responsibilities. You will be more clear in your mind and will get better results if you talk things over for the good of all concerned. Illness may bring a care or expense. Money affairs can be adjusted for general benefit, but will be slow. Enjoy old friends, maintain peaceful relationships, deepen your love and create harmony at home.

Personal Year Number Nine

You are deeply conscious in your mind and heart that you are done with someone or something. Examine the opinions of others carefully and think before speaking. Find time to be on your own for quiet thinking, but enjoy philosophical discussions. Let go of anything that wants to get away. Poise, inner calm and spiritual attraction will take care of everything. Take time to rest and relax.

Month: August

Universal Month Number Eight

In this month we look for substantial growth. Large plans are put into action. Business promotion and success are on the horizon.

Personal Year Number One

page 226

Take time to think over your plans; any delays are part of the normal flow. The new direction you're thinking of will need more time for it to fully work out. Always focus on a positive attitude. You have changed; therefore be patient and feel confident. For best result show kindness and understanding in your interactions with others. Travel, and join friends in humanitarian interests.

Personal Year Number Two

You may feel more philosophical and spiritual, and because of this will become aware what you want from life – your own purpose and happiness. This might surprise you, but will guide you to get ready for a new start and a new relationship in the future. However refuse to act in any way that will force issues of the past and cause you regrets. Be careful and use diplomacy in what you say and do.

Personal Year Number Three

Moves or changes in living conditions may take place or be considered. There will be pleasant social contact with friends and you will find help there if needed. For best results this month be agreeable and cooperative, and show patience in all circumstances. There are many small duties to take care of, which will free you up from responsibility. Partnerships can change or end and new interests can be developed.

Personal Year Number Four

This is the best time to get a bit of fun out of life or go on holiday. Spend a little money on yourself, but don't be extravagant. Business may still be slow, but the possibility to make some money is there as well. It's a time to make new friends and you could meet people who will mean a lot to your future. Find some new ideas of a creative and artistic nature, but be careful about talking out of turn.

Personal Year Number Five

You have a strong desire for freedom, life and progress. This is a good time to be practical about plans, clear away the obstacles, take the responsibility and get things in better order. Money may be needed – you may feel limited – but go after results and you will be successful. Be smart with competitors and work out your own problems. Take care of your health and make positive changes if needed.

Personal Year Number Six

Take care of all personal and business legal matters. Make sure that even the small things you do will in some way benefit others and be for the good of all. Move forward; people will be coming and going and you may be travelling or going places too. You will be excited and pleased. There is still much to keep you busy and on the job – some duty is still present as well. Look after your health.

Personal Year Number Seven

Express a lot of sympathy for others and help them with their problems. If there is a stalemate with your plans, just go back to your studies – your reading – and relax and enjoy simple pleasures. The family will keep you busy, give much pleasure and be interesting, especially through children or younger people. A restriction may be present, but you should not mind this; instead talk things over.

Personal Year Number Eight

You may feel alone, but it's best to say very little. Don't worry – everything will work out all right of its own accord. Take some rest and relax; even a little trip would do a lot of good. Take up a new study, do a few things that make you happy. Watch your diet too, for your health's sake. Use your good business ability and good judgement. Have faith and keep poised and all will work out satisfactorily.

Personal Year Number Nine

Move forward in a dynamic, businesslike way – you feel more empowered. This will clear the way for the future. Love affairs – yours or those of others – could play a part, but be wise enough not to become involved unless you are sure. You should have a reward or recognition or some kind of honour this month. Put yourself into general business affairs and show executive ability.

Notes

page 229

Month: September

Universal Month Number Nine

In this month we take stock, eliminate, and put things in order. Public personalities are discovered.

Personal Year Number One

page 230

This is a good time to rest and to have your annual health check-up. You will need to show more tact, diplomacy and cooperation in new associations. The new plan will take most of your time, energy and goodwill now. Do not neglect your duties or the tasks at hand. Hold on to your position and make few demands; much has been accomplished. You have great inner strength, courage and willpower right now.

Personal Year Number Two

This month enjoy short trips, friends and family and be part of social activities. This year will have given you the opportunity to show your talents for cooperation and you will have been given more authority. There is less need for patience now; instead, appreciate what you have gained and keep a quiet inner poise. Progress and results depend a great deal upon your character, so be the sensitive, positive type.

Personal Year Number Three

This month maintain your self-control and keep a positive attitude. Also seek spiritual help and business counsel. Involve yourself in cultural activities and explore new networking opportunities. A personal plan can now be carried out and more fully realised. You must retain the right mental attitude and an optimistic point of view, and not be afraid to move forward. Always avoid blaming others.

Personal Year Number Four

This month refuse to let anything get you down. Instead take stock of what you have accomplished with satisfaction and be thankful for all the hard work done. Keep your goals in mind and focus on the details. Take a little time out, eat properly for the sake of your health and keep to an exercise routine. Your efforts have provided you with experience, security and a business opportunity for the future.

Personal Year Number Five

This is a good time to take up new things, to advertise, to make public contacts, to move and to make general improvements. Just go forward in a constructive and wise manner; avoid making hasty decisions. You have set yourself free from some old condition or responsibility so go with the new, but use good judgment in all opportunities for growth and change. Take a trip if you feel like it.

Personal Year Number Six

You will feel much duty and responsibility. Love affairs, marriages, divorces and all manner of human problems may touch your life. This will give you the chance to give wise counsel and to bring justice to the situations that come up. Love and service to home, work, children and humanity will give the best results. Health matters still demand attention and care.

Personal Year Number Seven

The law of attraction is working for you and is the best method to use to get things done. It is necessary that you keep control of conditions and be poised. Take a trip for a rest or for a change, and work for inner peace and faith, which gives much personal growth. Watch your health. Keep your mind and heart happy and your body rested, and keep constructively busy. Read an inspirational book.

Personal Year Number Eight

You realise that you have truly accomplished financial improvement and general advancement through your mental and practical efforts. You may feel an inner unrest; do not turn away from true love or friendship for the sake of money or possessions. The focus this month is more on career than family. However you are gaining wisdom and learning the worth of right action over personal feelings.

Personal Year Number Nine

Life is moving forward and you should plan for the future. You will be emotional and will do much thinking and remembering, but the past must be put behind you. Focus on release and completion. You might feel some sorrow for what you have given up or finished, even though this was necessary. You should feel satisfaction in the results of your past efforts. Be generous with your time to others.

Month: October

Universal Month Number One (10th)

This month has more force than single numbered month. In this month we introduce and get started on our new plans and ideas. Pioneers and inventors are discovered. Leaders are appointed. New committees are formed.

Personal Year Number One

This month you will have to show patience and diplomacy. Pay attention to details. You will be busy due to social activities, but these will all be to your advantage because there is a need to keep in touch with people. Reconnect with those who are close to you. However be wise – keep your own counsel. You are more sensitive and intuitive than usual. A new friendship or romance could now develop.

Personal Year Number Two

It is important you spend some time with yourself or with a few friends. Take some time out for the arts, or a movie. You will feel more creative, playful and optimistic. Progress will come in due time. Think about what you want to do – maybe have a holiday or take up a study. Your future should be carefully considered. Take care of your health. Reach out to people who inspire you.

Personal Year Number Three

The time has come to execute and carry out plans, so be practical. Your hard work will pay off with tangible results next year. You carry much responsibility. Take good care to have all contracts and agreements in sound order. Stay positive, enthusiastic, focused, and committed to the task at hand. Look after your health – eat well, exercise and take time to rest.

Personal Year Number Four

This is a month for changes, new interests, new work and new people. You will feel more free and relieved. It is a good time to promote yourself and your business. Be flexible and open-minded. You should enjoy many interesting experiences. Avoid arguments and hasty decisions because they could cause problems. You might have to work with young people and children.

Personal Year Number Five

You will have obligations to be met and must be helpful to others – this is not a time to be selfish. Family matters become more in the forefront. Plan a family get-together. People may ask favours of you and you will find pleasure in being helpful to others. An emotional problem seems to be present, but you are prepared to care for it in your own mind and in your own way.

Personal Year Number Six

Take time this month to rest, relax and be still – to read, study, and look at life from its deeper side. Reflect on the progress you've made so far, then review and adjust your goals for better results in view of new developments. Stay positive, keep your inner poise and faith, and be willing to accept help. Look for ways to improve your family life. Eat healthily and do not worry.

Personal Year Number Seven

Business affairs and property call for attention and good judgement. A business offer and a chance to get rid of some old conditions are likely this month. Excellent progress can be made in business now. You have grown stronger in understanding, confidence and self-knowledge. You may begin to sense the business goal of next year. First, though, take care of the things at hand.

Personal Year Number Eight

There is a demand for love, tolerance and compassion – otherwise someone or something may go out of your life, which could bring regret later. Bring longstanding projects to a close. You may experience a sense of loss. Try to focus on others rather than on yourself. Be generous. It is a good time to be done with any possession or circumstance that has outlived its usefulness.

Personal Year Number Nine

This month new interests, new people and something helpful and beneficial through others are present. Think things through first – there must be mutual benefit. Be ready to replace old ways of doing things with new, but don't rush into long-term commitments yet. The transition will occur gradually, there's no need to jump ahead of yourself. Instead look after yourself well, enjoy life and take some rest.

Notes

page 234

Month: November

Universal Month Number Two (11th)

This month has more force than single numbered month. In this month we collect materials and compile statistics. We use diplomacy and tact in politics.

Universal Month Number 11/2

This month has more force than the single-numbered month. In this month there will be activity in cults, churches, temples, synagogues and missions. Spiritual values will be expressed.

Personal Year Number One

An inspirational and creative month. You will feel optimistic and positive. Meet up with friends, buy things you need – even do some Christmas shopping – but stay within your budget. Have some fun – go to a social event, dinner party or a sports game. However try to stay focused on your goals; don't scatter your energies. Make time for new ideas and interests, and also enjoy your achievements.

Personal Year Number Two

A practical month – get down to work and do what must be done. You need to be organised and focus on the tasks at hand. Hard work will see results. Be especially wise in regard to papers, contracts and agreements. Study ways and means to get things done – look at the details. Take care of your health and don't worry. Children are part of the responsibility this month.

Personal Year Number Three

This is an active month for progress, experiencing new interests, or studying. Take a trip, socialise or move if you feel like it. Resist making impulsive decisions or the urge to run away. You might have some unexpected happening; use it to your advantage and you will achieve good results. Business should show improvement because of your own resourcefulness. Keep some free time for just you and be patient.

Personal Year Number Four

Try not to worry this month though the need for money is present because of responsibilities in your home and business. Be kind, understanding and sympathetic as you try to give service to others. Keep working on your plans for the future even if you feel a little uncertain about some of them. This year you had to make a start and set the pattern for next year. Take care of your health – eat well and exercise.

Personal Year Number Five

This is a time to take a rest and be alone for a while, enjoying the peace and quiet. Take time to think and work out in your mind how to go forward with all the changes that have been happening. Meditate and connect with your inner self. A deep understanding will be gained, which will help you to take care of all your problems. Stay in tune with the needs of the people you love. Take care of yourself and your health.

Personal Year Number Six

Gain harmony in all relationships. Meet with people who are successful this will bring you assistance in business. This is a rewarding time; put your focus on the results that are happening. Money should be managed or acquired through service and through the influence you have gained during this year. Houses and property are to be considered, but always be businesslike.

Personal Year Number Seven

Many things in your life will be adjusted and will reach a new level. The best approach will be in showing compassion and forgiveness to others. Volunteer some time and energy to the community. Focus on others rather than on yourself. If the way is not all clear and you are not absolutely sure of the future, contemplate the higher ideals and you will experience many blessings and rewards.

Personal Year Number Eight

This is a busy month, with clarity in regard to property, business and love affairs. You will see beginnings and endings. You should be conscious of a new way of thinking or work, which will bring much interest and inspiration. There is no need to make rash decisions; take your time and balance your enthusiasm with sensitivity. Health issues need to be taken seriously; give yourself a health check-up.

Personal Year Number Nine

This will be a pleasant month. A lot is happening under the surface, so show patience with your project and desire. Wait for feedback and be flexible. Quietly hold on to your plans and wishes; cooperation will work to your advantage. You may meet and spend some quality time with old friends. Other people will depend on you a lot; this will keep you busy in spite of some delay. Find some quiet time for yourself.

Month: December

Universal Month Number Three (12th)

This month has more force than single numbered month. In this month we find activity in the market. Look for amusements, fun and friends. You will be busy operating committees.

Personal Year Number One

This is a time to strengthen your foundations – get down to work and face all your responsibilities in business, social and general circumstances. Pay close attention to details, order and schedules. You will see some results or progress in your plans. Take care of your health. Make others happy – give some attention to home and family. Look back over the year and recognise it has been good after all.

Personal Year Number Two

This is an exciting month with lots of variety, surprises, travel and new friends. A good time to be flexible, to promote your business or yourself. You have a feeling of freedom and self-confidence; you must be assertive, but avoid arguments. Take care of important matters first. Be helpful. Look back over the year and know you have learned to show patience and cooperation, and have been diplomatic.

Personal Year Number Three

This is a great month to enjoy a holiday with family and friends. It is your responsibility to be of service to others. You will find little time for yourself. Your attention will be directed at home, dinner parties, social gatherings and Christmas with close relatives. Any love affairs and emotional matters are to be considered and enjoyed. You may be ready to commit to a long-term relationship.

Personal Year Number Four

This month you will reconnect with your inner spirit. You need some time by yourself to reflect, re-evaluating your situation and your long-term goals. This is not your duty Christmas; have faith in yourself and in things in general. Keep your poise and avoid worry and an improvement will come about, making the year much nicer than you had thought possible. Enjoy some peaceful time in nature.

Personal Year Number Five

You will enjoy more freedom and your focus will be more on money and business. You will feel more confident and empowered than you have been in a long time. Christmas will be pleasant and interesting. Trips for pleasure and business are possible. You should realise that the year has been one of great importance and that you are now free from many of the old problems.

Personal Year Number Six

This is a time to relieve yourself of clutter and finish home projects. You do not need to carry too much Christmas responsibility. You could be alone or conditions may not be as they usually are. The month will bring settlements, completions, and something pleasing in the way the year has turned out. You are much happier concerning home and family. Take a vacation and have some rest.

Personal Year Number Seven

This month will be busy and different in some respects. You will feel more energised and are ready to make some changes in your life. Avoid making hasty decisions and focus on short-term goals. Look for a trip, visitors and the unexpected, but with more freedom and new interests. Make Christmas a pleasant time and prepare yourself to take advantage of business opportunities next year.

Personal Year Number Eight

A good time to reflect and take a little time out. You will feel sensitive and a little vulnerable. Enjoy Christmas and take time for pleasant little things and happy social activities. You could feel a touch tired after your busy year. If you have been true to yourself and have lived up to your best character you will gain much satisfaction and feel the work has all been worthwhile.

Personal Year Number Nine

This month celebrate and share good times with friends and family. Good news is coming. Be creative and entertain others in order to enjoy life. Have fun, party with friends, take a vacation or travel. This month is a time to do pleasant things. An opportunity may present itself for you to express your talents and artistic ability but there is no need to rush into things. You've earned your time out.

Notes

page 242

page 243

Self-empowerment

Whatever you can do,

or dream

You can,

begin it.

Boldness has genius,

power

and magic in it;

Begin it now.

Johann Wolfgang von Goethe

Chapter 22

Personal days 1-9, 11/2, 22/4 and Universal

Our personal day also carries an energy, that can be calculated into a number, and this will guide you how to best direct yourself in the day – your daily life. I believe it is also very important to take the Universal energy for the day into account as well. Your Personal Day doesn't work alone; the Universal Day must be carefully considered before acting on decisions in your daily life. Then we will have a better chance of taking opportunities and being successful. It is also a great way for us to avoid disappointments or failures in our everyday life.

Your Personal Day is calculated by adding the Personal Year to the Calendar Month and the Calendar Day.

For example: your **Personal Year** is 7, the **Calendar Month** is December (12th month adds up to 3), Christmas Day (25th December) is the **Calendar Day** 2 + 5 = 7.

7(PY) + 3(CM) + 7(CD) = 17 continue to reduce 1 + 7 = 8

Therefore Christmas Day will have the personal vibration of number eight for you in your Personal Year seven. Find on pages 248 to 250 the detail for every Personal Day in all Personal Years

The details for Personal Day 11/2 found in February and Personal Day 22/4 in April.

Always reduce everything to single digits, except the numbers 11 and 22.

The Universal Day is found by adding the **Universal Year** to the **Calendar Month** and the **Calendar Day**.

For example: Universal Year 2013 (2 + 1 + 3 = 6), the Calendar Month is December (12th month adds up to 3), Christmas Day is the Calendar Day 2 + 5 = 7

6(UY) + 3(CM) + 7 (CD) = 16 continue to reduce 1 + 6 = 7

Therefore Christmas Day in 2013 will have the Universal vibration of number seven for everyone.

Find on pages 248 to 250 the detail for every Universal Day in the nine year cycle.

The details for Personal Day 11/2 found in February and Personal Day 22/4 in April.

Always reduce everything to single digits, except the numbers 11 and 22.

As you live your life and follow your own personal direction for the day, also take the Universal vibration of the Calendar Day into account. This will have an influence on you as well.

We can never forget the Universal vibration, which is always around us and has a significant impact on our lives. We must always understand and integrate both our Personal and Universal vibration. As an example in Christchurch the Universal energy caused the natural disaster, which has a great impact on your daily, monthly and yearly life. However we make our own lives, decide our own choices, and if we live on the positive side of our own personal vibration we can live our own very Best Life and have everything we could possibly want.

Universal Day Number 1

Time for new ideas. Powerful market. Forceful public opinion.

Personal Day Number 1

A good day to put new plans into action. No more delays – you must start. Go after the new career. Keep your important purpose in mind and make every effort to start the process. Show commitment. Step up, be original, and hold your own council. Go forward.

Universal Day Number 2

A quiet day. Collecting and preparing for the following day. Slow movement.

Personal Day Number 2

A day for cooperation – listen to the opinions of another person. Be the peacemaker. A pleasant, but quiet day. Not a good day to change plans. Stay balanced and move forward smoothly. Do something for someone. Collect information, facts or things.

Universal Day Number 11/2

This day is like number 2, but its emphasis is on spirituality.

Personal Day Number 11/2

This is a day to go within yourself and seek understanding and sensitivity. Be a comfort, if anyone seems to want or need it. Take time to look for the vision ahead. Business and the making of money is to be dismissed from one's mind or thoughts. Slow down, force no issues.

Universal Day Number 3

This day is experienced as a lot of nervous energy and scattered forces. The market is erratic. An active, pleasure-seeking day.

Personal Day Number 3

Have a good time today – laugh, sing, refuse to worry. Visit friends, entertain, be social. Do your shopping, write your thoughts down on paper, be creative. A happy go-easy day.

Universal Day Number 4

This day we pay attention to schedules and details. We find a steadier market. We may experience turning points.

Personal Day Number 4

A day to be serious, work hard, plan a schedule and get it done. Be focused. Any work that's already needed to be done for a long time, get it out of the way. Look at your budget and put your finances in order.

Universal Day Number 22/4

This day is like number 4, but with a stronger drive to create.

Personal Day Number 22/4

Today put your vision into working form. This is a day with much power potential and general improvement. Bring order and system into your big plans.

Universal Day Number 5

This is a day for freedom and expansion. You will experience group activities, go out to socialise with other people, and see plays and films.

Personal Day Number 5

Look for new ideas or change something today. You feel free and are willing to take a risk or a chance. Meet people or find members of the community, and know what's going on in the world. Do something different, out of the ordinary. Be adaptable and meet any emergency. Keep an open mind and look ahead.

Universal Day Number 6

You will enjoy your home today. Any arts or music is well attended. Join in group activities.

Personal Day Number 6

Today enjoy your home and family. Check if any work around the house is needed, and attend to family members and friends. Cook a beautiful meal. Make any calls you should make. Give out as much love, friendship and harmony as you are able. Look after yourself and love yourself.

Universal Day Number 7

This is the day the market sees improvements. We analyse and are looking for inner peace.

Personal Day Number 7

Find time for yourself to be alone and rest. Meditate, find inner peace. Analyse the last few days and weeks. Take time to think and be poised. Perfect everything you are doing. Seek nothing for yourself, your family or your business.

Universal Day Number 8

This day you will experience big success. Company executive meetings are scheduled.

Personal Day Number 8

A personal power day when much can be accomplished. You will have maximum impact in business and financial matters. Consider the possibilities, but move forward. Keep your aim in mind – it's a great day for material gain and advancement.

Universal Day Number 9

Today you must consider public affairs and humanitarian ventures. Work on friendly relationships and aim for more tolerance.

Personal Day Number 9

A day for brotherhood; forget your personal wishes. This is a time for completion, to finish your tasks. Show goodwill and act with an awareness of others' needs and desires; bear no grudges. Much drama and emotion may be felt through endings. Understanding and compassion will be needed in all situations.

Miss me, but let me go

When I come to the end of the road,
and the sun has set for me.
I want no rites in a gloom-filled room.
Why cry for a soul set free?
Miss me a little but not too long,
and not with your head bowed low.
Remember the love that was once shared.
Miss me, but let me go.

For this is a journey we all must take,
and each must go alone.
It's all a part of the master's plan,
a step on the road to home.
When you are lonely and sick of heart,
go to the friends we know.
Bear your sorrow in good deeds.
Miss me, but let me go.

Author unknown

Chapter 23

Lucky numbers

page 256

The day we are born is our lucky day, we were given life. Every day is a lucky day, but the day that provides the lucky date will bring success. The number of our day and the support of the sun sign, the Astrological influence, of the birth day play a powerful role in understanding its significance and the explaining of its vibration. There is a powerful influence exerted by the Sun 1 and the Moon 2, along with the other planets Jupiter 3, Uranus 4, Mercury 5, Venus 6, Neptune 7, Saturn 8, Mars 9 and the constellations (a group of fixed stars whose outline is traditionally regarded as forming a particular figure, e.g. Milky Way a faintly luminous band of light emitted by countless stars encircling the heavens; the Galaxy). There are twelve Astrological Sun signs, each exerting an influence, that lasts for a period averaging one calendar month. It takes Earth a full calendar year to go around its Sun. There are four elements Fire, Earth, Air and Water.

Aries	March 21st – April 20th	Element Fire
Taurus	April 21st – May 20th	Element Earth
Gemini	May 21st – June 2th	Element Air
Cancer	June 21st – July 21st	Element Water
Leo	July 22nd – August 22nd	Element Fire
Virgo	August 23rd – September 22nd	Element Earth
Libra	September 23rd – October 22nd	Element Air
Scorpio	October 23rd – November 22nd	Element Water
Sagittarius	November 23rd – December 22nd	Element Fire
Capricorn	December 23rd – January 21st	Element Earth
Aquarius	January 22nd – February 20th	Element Air
Pisces	February 21st – March 20th	Element Water

Count Louis Hamon, better known under the name Cheiro. He was a popular and influential seer and lived early in the twentieth century. He was an eminent palmist, astrologer and numerologist. He studied the nature of the relationship between numbers and letters from many different angles. He achieved great success in his life and many disinguished people consulted him. His list of famous people included Sir Arthur Sullivan, Mark Twain, H.H. The Infanta Eulalia, General Sir Redvers Buller, Rt. Hon. Sir. Austen Chamberlain, Lord Leighton, Dame Nellie Melba. He died in 1936, he left behind him a number of remarkable books, the total sales of which throughout the world must now run into millions. I was given his book, *Cheiro's Book of Numbers*, on two occasions – one time for me to read and the other time for me to keep. I see this as significant and important and decided to include some of his information in this book. He has done a lot of research in the lucky day vibration. The influence of colours and numbers go together.

I strongly believe in vibration and the importance of tapping into the best energies for yourself at the best time possible. I use this information myself in everything important that I do.

Have fun with it and see if you can benefit and create more good luck in your OWN Best Life. I'm grateful for feedback for research purposes. Thank you in advance.

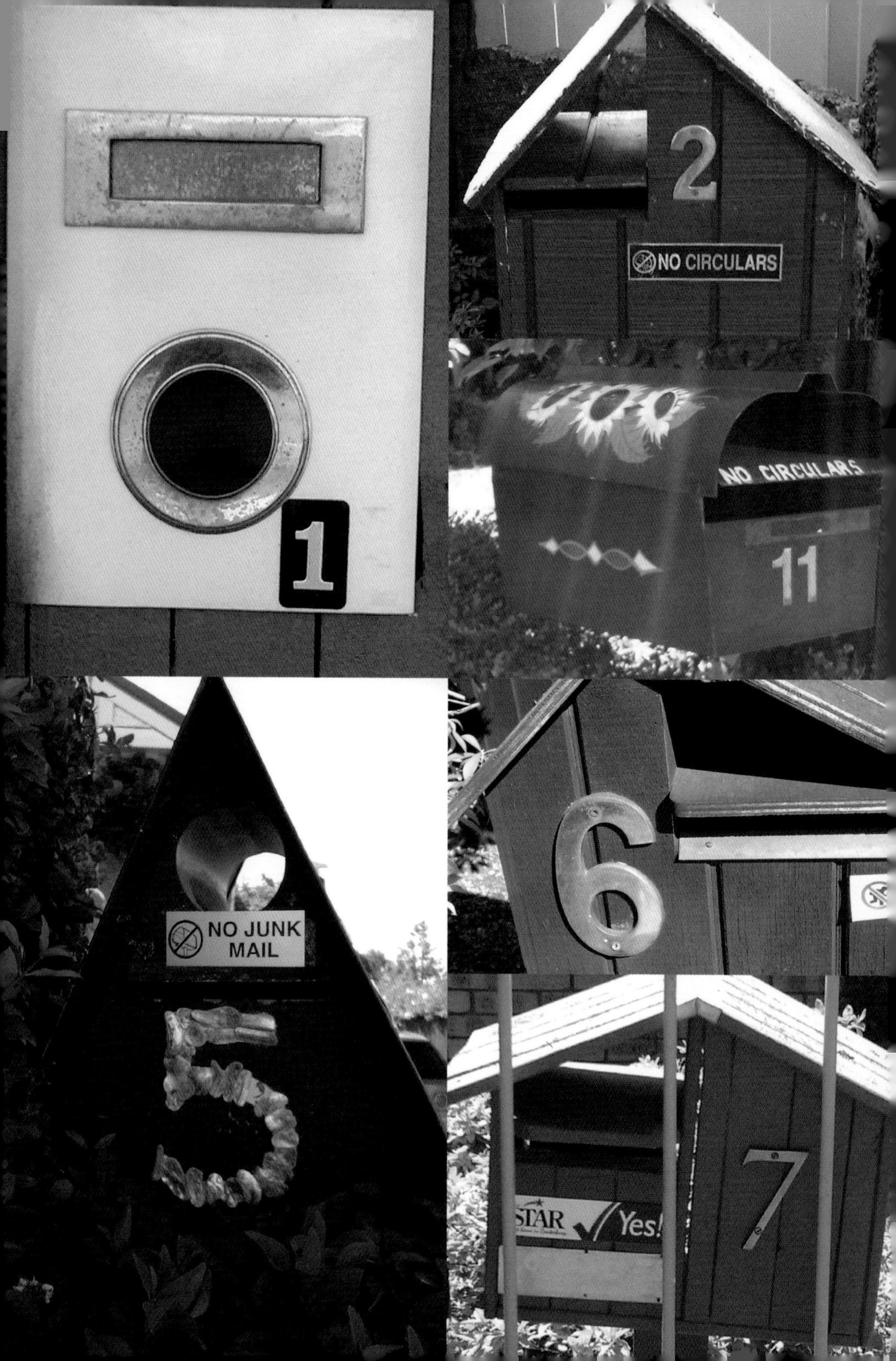
1
2
NO CIRCULARS
NO CIRCULARS
11
NO JUNK MAIL
5
6
STAR
Yes!
7

NO JUNK MAIL
4
Christchurch STAR Yes Please
4
3
22
8
NO CIRCULARS
9
IF I DON'T CALL THE POLICE MY NEIGHBOUR WILL
Christchurch STAR Yes Please
NO CIRCULARS

Birth Number 1-10-19-28

A person born with the Birth Number 1-10-19-28 of any month should carry out their most important plans and ideas on the day that vibrates to their own number – especially during the period from 21 July to 28 August and from 21 March to 28 April.

The days of the week most lucky for Number 1 people are Sunday and Monday, especially if their own number should fall on one of those days.

Lucky colours for the person born under Number 1 are all shades of gold – yellow, sandal and bronze to golden brown.

Their lucky stones are topaz, amber, yellow diamond and all other stones of these colours. If possible they should wear a piece of amber next to their skin.

Birth Number 2-11-20-29

A person born with Birth Number 2-11-20-29 of any month should carry out their most important plans and ideas on the days that vibrate with their own number, especially during the period from 20 June to 27 July.

The days of the week that are the most lucky for Number 2 people are Sunday, Monday and Friday, particularly if their own number should fall on one of those days.

The lucky colours for the person born under Number 2 are all shades of green – from the darkest to the lightest – plus cream and white. They should avoid all dark colours, especially black, purple and dark red.

Their lucky jewels are pearls, cat's eye, tiger's eye, jade, moonstones and pale green stones. They should always carry a piece of jade with them, and if possible wear it next to their skin.

Birth Number 3-12-21-30

A person born with Birth Number 3-12-21-30 of any month should carry out their most important plans and ideas on the days that vibrate with their number, especially during the periods from 19 February to March 20-27 and from 21 November to December 20-27.

The days of the week that are luckier for Number 3 people are Thursday, Friday and Tuesday; Thursday being the most important and especially if their own number should fall on one of those days.

The lucky colours for the person born under Number 3 are some shade of mauve, yellow, sandal, gold, orange, violet or purple. Some touch of these colours should always be with them; also in the rooms in which they live. All shades of blue, crimson and rose are also favourable to them, but more as secondary colours.

Their lucky stone is amethyst. They should always carry a piece with them and if possible wear it next to their skin.

Birth Number 4-13-22-31

A person born with Birth number 4-13-22-31 of any month should carry out their most important plans and ideas on the days that vibrate with their number, especially during the periods from 21 June to July 20-27 and from 22 July to the end of August.

The days of the week that are more lucky for Number 4 people are Saturday, Sunday and Monday, particularly if their own number falls on one of those days.

The lucky colours the person born under Number 4 should wear are called half-shades; pale blue, sky blue, yellow, sandal and gold or electric colours. Electric blues and greys seem to suit them best of all.

Their lucky stone is sapphire – light or dark, opal and blue acquamarine. If possible they should wear this stone next to their skin.

Birth Number 5-14-23

A person born with Birth Number 5-14-23 of any month should carry out their most important plans and ideas on the days that vibrate with their number, especially during the periods from 21 May to June 20-27 and from 21 August to September 20–27.

The days of the week that are luckier for Number 5 people are Wednesday and Friday, particularly if their own number falls on one of those days.

Their lucky colours are all shades of light grey, pale blue, white, gold, silver and glistening materials. They are lucky in that they can wear all shades of colour, but by far the best for them are light shades and they should wear dark colours as rarely as possible.

Their lucky stone is the diamond, zircon plus all glittering or shimmering things; also ornaments made of platinum or silver. If possible they should wear a diamond set in platinum next to their skin.

Birth Number 6-15-24

A person born with Birth Number 6-15-24 of any month should carry out their most important plans and ideas on the days that vibrate with their number, especially during the periods from 20 April to May 20-27 and from 21 September to October 20–27.

The days of the week that are luckier for Number 6 people are Tuesday, Thursday and Friday, particularly if their own number falls on one of those days.

Their lucky colours are green, shades of blue, from the lightest to the darkest, and also all shades of rose or pink, but they should avoid wearing black or dark purple.

Their lucky stones are jade, green aquamarine and especially the turquoise and the emerald. If possible they should wear a turquoise or a piece of turquoise matrix next to their skin.

Birth Number 7-16-25

A person born with Birth Number 7-16-25 of any month should carry out their most important plans and ideas on the days that vibrate with their number, especially during the period from 21 June to July 20-27 and less strongly from that date until the end of August.

The days of the week that are luckier for Number 7 people are Sunday and Monday, particularly if their own number falls on one of those days.

page 266

Their lucky colours are all shades of green, blue, pale yellow and white. They should avoid all heavy, dark colours as much as possible.

Their lucky stones are moonstones, opal, jade, tiger's eyes, cat's eyes and pearls. If possible they should wear a moonstone or a piece of moss against their skin.

Birth Number 8-17-26

A person born with Birth Number 8-17-26 of any month should carry out their most important plans and ideas on the days that vibrate with their number, especially during the period 21 December to January 20-27th, and from 27 January to February 19–26th. The first mentioned period is the Positive of their number, while the second is the Negative.

The days of the week that are luckier for Number 8 people are Saturday (most important), Sunday and Monday, particularly if their own number falls on one of those days.

Their lucky colours are all shades of dark grey, black, yellow, gold, sandal, purple, blue and dark blue.

Their lucky stones are blue carbuncle: indira blue is best, amethysts, blue aquamarine and dark-toned sapphires, the black pearl, or the black diamond. If possible they should wear one of these against their skin.

Birth Number 9-18-27

A person born with Birth Number 9-18-27 of any month should carry out their most important plans and ideas on the days that vibrate with their number, especially during the periods from 21 March to April 19-26 and from 21 October to November 20-27.

The days of the week that are luckier for Number 9 people are Tuesday (most important), Thursday and Friday, particularly if their own number falls on one of those days.

Their lucky colours are blue, yellow, white, all shades of crimson or light and dark red, and also all rose tones and pinks.

Their lucky stones are the ruby, opal (red), garnet, coral (best red) and bloodstone. If possible they should wear one of these stones next to their skin.

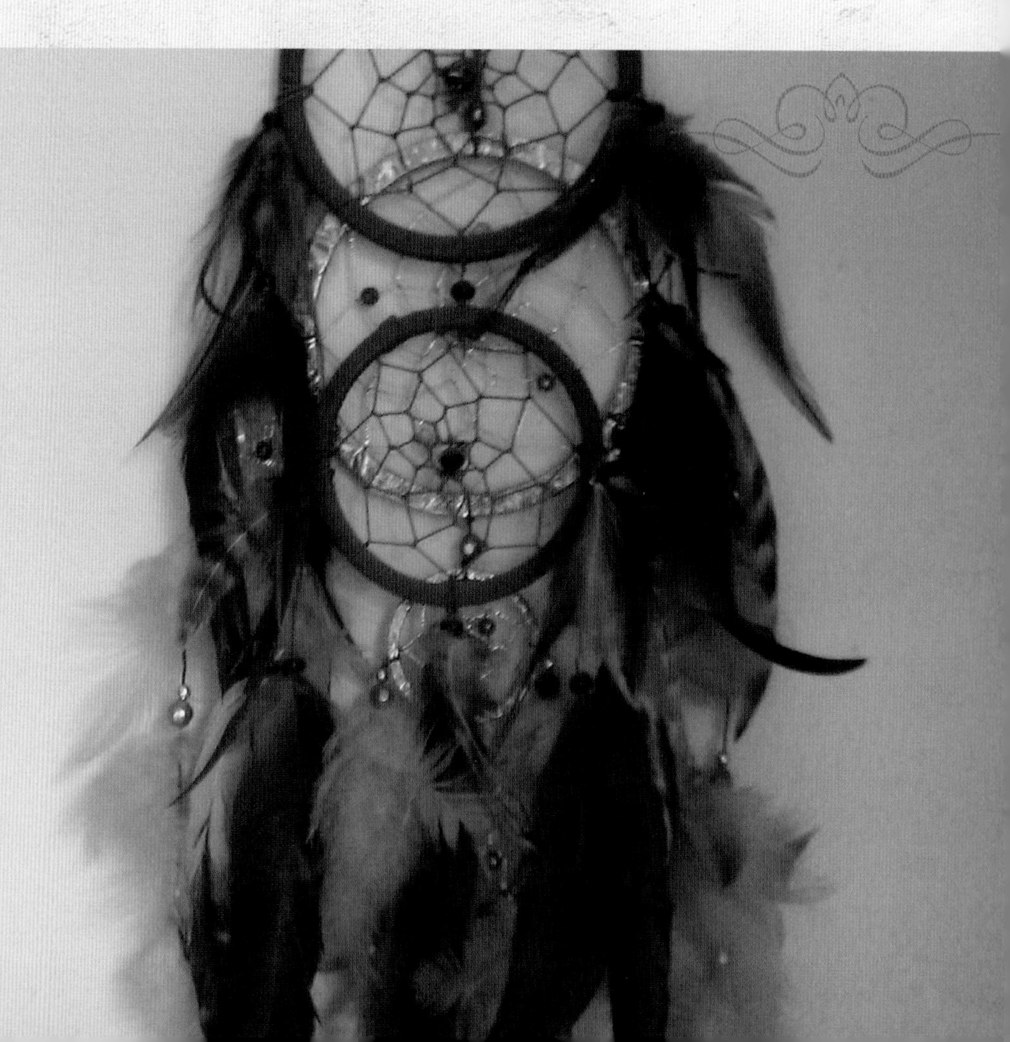

Never discourage anyone

Never discourage anyone,
who continually makes progress,
no matter how slow.

Plato

Bibliography

General

Mountain Dreamer, Oriah, *The Invitation*. HarperCollins, HarperSanFrancisco 1999, New York.

Hill, Napoleon, *Think and Grow Rich*, The Ralston Society 1937, Meriden, Conn.

Hicks, Esther and Jerry, *Ask and It Is Given (on the teachings of Abraham)*, Hay House, Inc. 2004, Australia by Griffin Press.

Law Nolte, Dorothy, *Children Learn What They Live*, Workman Publishing Co. Inc.1998, New York.

Dan, Yu, *Confucius From The Heart*, Zhonghua Book Co. 2006, UK CPI Mackays, Chatham.

Williamson, Marianne, *Everyday Grace*, Bantam Books 2003, Great Britain, Clays Ltd, Bungay, Suffolk.

Winfrey, Oprah, *Words that Matter*, Harper Studio 2010, New York.

Ehrmann, Max, *Desiderata*, Random House New Zealand Ltd 2002.

Maher, Suzanne, *Eternity (Affirmations)*, Australia Pty Ltd 2006, Bellingen NSW.

Hay, Louise L, *You Can Heal Your Life*, Hay House, Inc. 1984, Concord, N.S.W. Australia.

Tolle, Eckhart, *The Power of Now*, Hodder Headline Australia Pty Ltd 2000, Sydney.

Dyer, Dr. Wayne W., *The Power of Intention*, Hay House, Inc. 2004, Carlsbad, CA.

Carnegie, Dale, *How to Win Friends and Influence People*, Vermilion London 1998.

Kiyosaki, Robert T, *Rich Dad Poor Dad*, TechPress, Inc. 1997, Paradise Valley, AZ.

Covey, Stephen R, *The 7 Habits of Highly Effective People*, Simon & Schuster Inc.1989, Australia.

Scheinfeld, Robert, *Busting Loose from the Money Game*, John Wiley & Sons, Inc. 2006, Hoboken, New Jersey.

Grabhorn, Lynn, *Excuse Me, Your Life Is Waiting*, Hampton Roads Publishing Co. Inc, 2000, London.

Richardson, Cheryl, *Take Time for Your Life*, Bantam Books 2000, London.

McGraw , Dr. Phillip C, *Life Strategies*, Vermilion London 1999.

Moore, Patrick, Sir, *Countdown! Or How Nigh Is the End?*, The History Press 2009, England.

Cooper, Diana, *2012 and Beyond*, Findhorn Press 2009, Scotland UK.

Harris, RN, Trudy, *Glimpses of Heaven*, Revell, a division of Baker Publishing Group 2008.

Numerology

Campbell, Florence, *Your Days Are Numbered*. The Gateway 1931, Marina del Rey, CA, USA.

Cheiro, *Cheiro's Book of Numbers*. Arco Publishing, Inc. 1964, London.

Decoz, Hans & Monte , Tom, *Numerology: Key to Your Inner Self*, Perigee Book, The Berkley Publishing Group 1994, New York.

Drayer, Ruth, *Numerology: The Power in Numbers*. Square One Publications 2003, New York.

Goodwin, Matthew Oliver, *Numerology: The Complete Guide – Volume 1, The Personality Reading*. Newcastle Publishing Company 1981, America.

Goodwin, Matthew Oliver, *Numerology: The Complete Guide – Volume 2, Advanced Personality Analysis and Reading the Past, Present, and Future*. Newcastle Publishing Company 2000, America.

Jordan, Juno, *The Romance In Your Name*. Rowny Press 1965, Camarillo, CA USA.

Lawrence, Shirley Blackwell, *The Secret Science of Numerology, The Hidden Meaning of Numbers and Letters*. New Page Books, division of The Career Press, Inc. 2001.

Lawrence, Shirley Blackwell, *Exploring Numerology, Life by the Numbers*. New Page Books, division of The Career Press, Inc. Franklin Lakes, NJ 2003.

Javane, Faith & Bunker, Dusty, *Numerology and the Divine Triangle*. Schiffer Publishing Ltd, 1979, Atglen PA, USA.

Bunker, Dusty, Numerology and Your Future. Whitford Press, division of Schiffer Publishing Ltd, Atglen, PA, USA 1980.

Too, Lillian, *168 Ways to Harness Your Lucky Numbers for Wealth, Success, and Happiness*. CICO Books, 2010, London.

Online resources numerology

www.numerology.org.uk – the official website of the *Association International de Numerologues*, incorporating the Connaissance School of Numerology

www.numbersru.com – Chaldean Numerology Charts and Readings since 1984

http://en.wikipedia.org/wiki/Numerology

www.numberquest.com

www.numerology.info.org

www.facade.com/numerology

www.bibletexts.com/glossary/number-symbolism.htm

www.psyche.com/psyche/qbl/comparative-numerology.html

Illustrations

Book and cover design: Leesa Ellis, **www.resolutiondesign.biz**

Author photo: Bryan Isbister from Creative Images Photography Ltd.

Photographs reprinted with permission as follows:
Jennifer Hay Front matter: rose, daisy, sunflower: page 6; pots, fountain, city, mushrooms: pages 50-58-79; broken crockery: page 80; red brick wall: pages 101-108-113-114/115-122-127-128-131-152/153-157-158/159-161-162-172-173-181-182-184-185-187-197-199-220-221-236/237

Kevin Hay Front matter: sunset-sunset bridge-pine cones; pages 1-2/3-4-5-10/11-12-13-14-15-20-21-22-23-24-28-29-31-32-36-37-38-39-40-44-45-46-52-56-63-68-69-70-73-76-77-82-84-88/89-93-97-104-142-145-146-148-149

Beth Adam Front matter: pink flower; pages 107-137-140/141-164/165-168/169-170-171-174-175-176-177-191-193-206-204-205-212-213-244-245-260-261
End matter: garages, sunset with boat

Nanny A. van den Oever: all other photos not credited above.

To write to the author

I would very much appreciate hearing from you and learning of your enjoyment of this book and how it has helped you. If you wish to contact me or would like more information about this book, please write to me at:

Nanny A. van den Oever
Best Life Ltd
74 Southampton Street
Sydenham
Christchurch 8023
New Zealand

Please send a self-addressed stamped envelope for reply. If you're outside New Zealand, please enclose an international postal reply coupon.

Best of Life is a book for yourself to keep or to give copies to those you love.

Sales / Distribution

Send e-mail to: **coaching@bestlife.co.nz**

Website: **www.bestlife.co.nz**

Order form

Distributed by:

Nanny A. van den Oever
Best Life Ltd,
74 Southampton Street,
Sydenham,
Christchurch 8023.
New Zealand.

Order book: *Best of Life*

Name: ____________________

Address: ____________________

Phone: ____________________

E-mail: ____________________

Price: $ ____________________

Date of order: ____________________

Order reference: ____________________

Quantity of order: ____________________

Postage and packaging: ____________________

Send to:

Name: ____________________

Address: ____________________

____

Phone: ____________________

E-mail: ____________________

By ordering direct from Best Life Ltd, you receive signed copies.

Mail order: submit through website: **www.bestlife.co.nz**

Enquiries e-mail: **coaching@bestlife.co.nz**

This book is available at quantity discounts for bulk purchases.

For information, please e-mail or call 64 3 337 3870